SKIMMING
STONES

SKIMMING STONES

STONES

and other ways
of being in the wild

Rob Cowen & Leo Critchley

CORONET

First published in Great Britain in 2012 by Coronet
An imprint of Hodder & Stoughton
An Hachette UK company

1

Copyright © Rob Cowen, Leo Critchley 2012

A CIP catalogue record for this title is available from the British Library

ISBN 978 1 444 73598 7

Printed and bound by Clays Ltd, St Ives plc

Hodder & Stoughton policy is to use papers that are natural, renewable
and recyclable products and made from wood grown in sustainable forests.
The logging and manufacturing processes are expected to conform
to the environmental regulations of the country of origin.

Hodder & Stoughton Ltd
338 Euston Road
London NW1 3BH

www.hodder.co.uk

Rob: For Rosie and my family.

Leo: For my family.

'After you have exhausted what there is in business, politics, conviviality, and so on – have found that none of these finally satisfy, or permanently wear – what remains? Nature remains.'

Walt Whitman

Contents

Introduction

Rob: My earliest memories are of forging a physical connection with the wild, chasing after my brother through the woods behind our house, over drystone walls and out on to the vast expanse of Ilkley Moor. It was an epic playground. Summer holidays seemed endless and were spent building dens, climbing trees, damming streams and sitting by campfires until the ring of our mum crashing a ladle around the inside of a saucepan signalled teatime. At seven years old, I knew the landscape around our house as well as I have known anything; the rough sandstone rocks, the taste of the hidden freshwater springs, the slithering of grass snakes in the bracken fields, and the unmistakable smell of purple-black bilberries in late summer. I can still remember that scent as it drifted across the lilac and green landscape like smoke, pooling in the bottom of the rocky crags and valleys. It was the unmistakable smell of belonging.

For a long time, however, I forgot it completely. My sights were set on becoming a professional writer and musician and I gravitated to the bright lights of London after university. Late nights singing in clubs were interspersed with early mornings rushing between offices or staring into the glare of a computer screen. My new cosmopolitan existence became necessarily hard-edged and urbanised, my view restricted by the sprawling mass of concrete and glass. After a year I no longer cared that my bedroom window faced a brick wall, as copy deadlines and responsibilities loomed larger in my mind; the stress of work and the pressure of juggling a life in three of the fastest paced industries in the world: journalism, PR and music. Success began to materialise but, contrary to what I imagined, it came with a mounting sense of alienation. My absorption into the urban had come with a price – I had lost my place in the wild. With it, I had lost a large part of myself too.

We forget that human beings are like every other animal, programmed to have a profound connection with nature and the natural world that surrounds us. It was an evolutionary necessity essential to our surviving and thriving and one that explains how we have managed to adapt to exist in some of the most inhospitable landscapes on this planet. We are born with this connection; it can be seen in the way every child delights in watching the wonders of nature. It remains every bit as important to our health and happiness as we grow older too, but, as I had found, the pressures of modern living can force our connection to fall by the wayside. We eat plastic-packaged food from around the globe, move from offices to gadget-filled homes in vehicles with tinted windows and climate control. We find ourselves too busy even to notice the seasons change unless it affects our commute to work.

Small wonder that in a recent poll conducted by the Natural History Museum, fewer than 25 per cent of Britons could identify a sycamore tree. Two-thirds were unable to recognise a peacock butterfly and 20 per cent couldn't put a name to an ammonite, one of our most common fossils. Ironically, in the struggle to try to establish a place in the world, we all too often cut ourselves off from our natural habitat.

Yet everybody instinctively knows nature is good for us. Why else would we pay more for hotel rooms with a view? Recent research confirms that hospital patients who can see trees and green space from their beds have been shown to recover more quickly than those who can't. Joggers who run through parks report feeling less anxious or depressed than people who do the same distance on a treadmill. The benefits of spending time in nature are rich indeed. There are forces deep in everyone's unconscious that find a pure expression in the simplest of activities enjoyed in the outdoors.

My rehabilitation started with day trips out to the countryside, doing the things I had done as a child, secreting myself in a wood to follow animal tracks or build a den. Soon I was enjoying a weekend of foraging wild food as I tramped over long-distance paths or slept out on the side of a snow-topped mountain. Each time, the transformative effect was powerful and tangible; stresses and worries fell away and were replaced with new ideas and inspiration. I always returned refreshed, renewed and ready to face the week ahead. Even when reporting on exotic shores as a travel journalist, I relished the return flight where I could press my face against the plane window as we descended through the clouds to survey the terrains below: the coasts, fields, woods, mountains and rivers. By the time we landed, I had already planned my next escape.

I started to carry this joy of reconnecting around with me in the form of literature, reading and re-reading writers who married the spiritual power of nature with tangible corporeal experience, J. A. Baker, Richard Jefferies, John Clare, Roger Deakin. These dog-eared books drew the attention of a blond-haired, scholarly lad working in the same office called Leo. At first I had avoided him as his jaw clicked when he ate his sandwiches and the books he was toting looked suspiciously like science fiction, but I quickly discovered that although we came from different backgrounds, we shared an obsession for landscapes both physical and literary that meant our lengthy discussions and reminiscences of holidays in the outdoors soon became the highlight of my working day. When he agreed to steal away and watch a sparrowhawk terrorise the

4

pigeons from the top-floor fire escape, I knew he was the perfect ally for my adventures.

Following our first trip together, which was back to the Yorkshire moors I wandered as a boy, we struck on the idea of writing a book that would act as an inspiration and a guide for everybody seeking the same sense of reconnection we were discovering. It seemed logical that we should share the simple techniques we can all practise that help us to really *be* in the terrains that lie outside our day-to-day lives, the seaside and coasts, the fields and forests, the mountains and rivers. Descending from the moors that day we started a journey that would change both our lives. I smelt the sweet scent of bilberries for the first time in years and I knew I belonged again.

Leo: In contrast to Rob, I was born and raised in London. Even at the furthest spot I have chosen to set my hat, Cambridge, I remained less than an hour's journey from the centre of the Big Smoke. But large portions of my family have lived or holidayed regularly in Cornwall since long before I was born. Nevertheless, I always felt a little out of place away from the sprawl where I grew up, whether it was being led by less inhibited cousins across seemingly endless muddy fields in the South West or camping with my uncles on the slopes of Kinder Scout.

Where landscape took root most deeply was in my mind. I formed a connection not with the land itself so much as the mood it could impart. As a child I was drawn to the littoral ribbon that lies across beaches between high and low tide. Encircled by pale sand and high cliffs, there were dark rocky protuberances, treacherous underfoot, sculpted into unworldly works of abstract art. The salt-smelling pools were full, too, of chance encounters with strange beings: anemones, limpets and mussels which clam up or clamp down at a touch; crabs, blennies and worms that would disappear under rocks or into the sand with a sudden frantic movement. The feeling of revelation that came, sitting by an apparently empty pool until eyes adjusted to see the creatures that re-emerged to go about their business. This was the feeling of entering another world.

When I studied literature at university, I was fascinated by our varied attempts to bring life to the landscape and the landscape into our psyches. *Poly-Olbion* is a long poem written by Drayton, a contemporary of Shakespeare. It is a poetical tour of the entire country that bathes the landscape in history and myths. It anthropomorphises entire counties, mountains and rivers, having them rise up and speak for themselves about their geography and their past. Few people regard it as a resounding success, but it is a rewarding experience to dip into it for a sense of how a particular area was viewed at the time, deepening our sense of the significance of a place.

Rob seemed something of a cultural collision when I first met him. We were working in a pretty straight-laced office, but he resolutely toted beaten-up cowboy boots – not a lace in sight. Tall and shaven-headed, he is an imposing figure for all of the five or six seconds it generally takes before he comes out with a childish joke.

When we first talked about our idea for a journey of reconnection and writing this book, I envisaged a kind of idyllic pastoral restorative. This illusion was dispelled, however, when we were driving up to our first jaunt on to the moors. Rob asked, 'Where are your walking boots?' I sheepishly explained that I only had work shoes and trainers to my name. To his credit, Rob only let a shimmer of doubt furrow his brow. As I dragged myself up the first steep slope, I knew I was being led again by someone much more comfortable there.

'This is harder than I thought,' I offered to the silhouette in front of me.

'That's what she said,' came the retort.

I was obliged to keep a careful eye out for boggier patches to avoid losing my trainers, which were fastened with Velcro and would not tighten sufficiently to prevent them coming loose. I was only able to look up and around momentarily, and the effort of the walk took much of my attention. After a while, however, the refreshing edge to the wind began to work on me. The exercise felt invigorating as I warmed up, and the chill of the air faded. It was still an alien land to me, but it was mine to explore.

As we fermented our thoughts about how we could share our experiences, this transformative effect became the touchstone for what we wanted to write. The 'How To' for each activity is explained so you can try it yourself, but it is supported by our reflections on why and how doing these activities has such a profound and important effect on us. There is also our digging up of the 'lore' relating to the land – historical and cultural odds and ends, as well as topics as broad as geology, myths and legends. This is knowledge our grandparents carried, but it is being lost.

Our hope is that you will be able to open this book on any chapter or even any page and find something to take away. Each chapter is also a narrative of our own experiences, which can be enjoyed from an armchair without needing to recreate them, but more adventurous readers may want to use the instructional elements as a basis for day trips and long weekends and all the facts and techniques are provided to enrich a personal experience.

Drayton said he wrote *Poly-Olbion* out of a sense of duty to Britain, and that he did not expect many to follow him on his imaginative quest. Our hope is the opposite: that you will ultimately discover a new side to yourself and be driven to uncover your own ways of being in the wild.

Seaside and Coasts

Skim a stone

In its most basic form, skimming stones involves nothing more than throwing a particular type of pebble into the water in a particular way so that instead of sinking it bounces or 'skips' across the surface. A tranquil stretch of seashore, the sort offered by a sheltered bay, is a good place to start.

Of course, no expensive equipment is required and the basic technique can be mastered quickly enough. Loosely hold a smooth, flattish, roundish stone measuring anything between 5 and 10 centimetres in diameter and about half a centimetre thick between the thumb and forefinger of your stronger hand. Tuck the other fingers underneath to take the weight, which should ideally be about the same as an egg (around 50 grams to 60 grams).

Take a moment to trace the proposed trajectory through the air. Imagine you are going to post the stone through a letterbox 3 metres offshore, angling your hand so the front of the stone is pointing slightly upwards. Keep the throwing elbow close to the body and swing the stone from hip height, whipping the hand around and driving the skimmer in as straight a line as possible. Velocity gives the stone the energy to keep going, but the trick is in the spin, ensuring the stone remains stable in flight after each impact and achieves the maximum number of skips. Grip any rough edge on the stone with the tip of the index finger and use it as a leverage point to start it spinning. At the moment of release your finger should point the stone on its way, but the complete action will carry your arm across the body, with your hand finishing almost at the opposite shoulder.

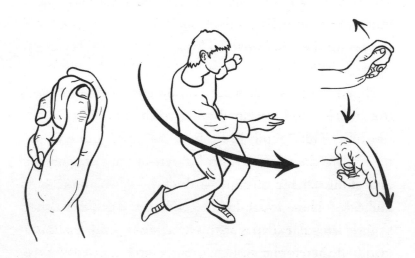

A good skimming throw has similarities with a good golf swing, the whole body working in concert. Balance and rhythm are vitally important; your weight should move in the direction of the throw, but never beyond the edges of your feet. This keeps you connected with the ground, so the energy of the throw pushes the stone forwards, rather than pushing you off-line. The linkage should be maintained all through the body, from ground to legs, legs to hips, hips to arms, arms to hands, and finally the fingers driving the stone.

By lifting the arm back behind your head or, for an extra flourish, attempting a run-up, you may achieve more power and greater distance, but it is essential to stay balanced at the moment of launch so you don't lose all that extra energy through poor technique. Always bring the stone down to hip-height in order to keep the angle low and the skipping smooth. Experiments suggest that a gradient of 20° between the stone's flight and the water is perfect for the first impact, but achieving this dead-on can be tricky. The best way to get the right 'feel' is through trial and error, as it depends on how hard you are throwing the stone and any environmental conditions like waves or wind. Every September hundreds of experts put the theories to the test when taking part in the annual Stone Skimming Championships on Easdale Island in the Inner Hebrides. These rough-handed devotees will tell you that slightly irregular shapes are preferable as they give a better grip and therefore spin faster, with some mavericks even carrying triangular stones.

Following a few warm-up movements, your time comes and the stone is released. It hangs above the water and all the world seems to pause, watching to see if it will pitty-pat triumphantly on its way towards the horizon or vanish with a derisory 'plop'. Regardless, one thing is certain, while you may need a few goes to pick up the knack, the satisfactions are well worth it: the first successful bounce, the first leaping of an incoming wave, the first series of five, now ten, now fifteen skips, all these can draw uncontrollable whoops of joy from somewhere deep inside the soul.

This power to delight hit us in the Highlands of Scotland one September a few years ago. At the eastern edge of the Knoydart peninsula the last road dwindles to nothing and we had set out on foot to negotiate 80 square miles of wilderness, hugging the eerily empty shore of Kinlochourn. Keeping the sea loch to the north, we had spent a day fighting our way through patches of scratchy heather and sharp gorse along rough, stony tracks no wider than a boot. There were no reassuring 'hellos' from fellow ramblers as we crunched up ascent after gruelling ascent. Only the echoes of our own shouts rang around the snow-topped munros. By mid-afternoon, we knew we wouldn't make it to the hamlet of Inverie, the only nod to civilisation on the peninsula and our proposed destination. Worse, it was too late to turn back; we could never reach the car before dark. There was only one option: to camp where we stood, on the only bit of flat ground around, next to a deserted sandy bay. A mix of excitement and nervousness rose in our stomachs at the thought of sleeping somewhere so isolated and far from help. We pitched our tent in the grass just off the beach and began to scout the immediate area, walking out across the shallow bluff and then back along the shore. Perhaps seeking some reassurance or distraction, we began idly throwing the odd pebble, but this quickly turned to something neither of us had done for a long time: skimming stones.

The best skimmers lay half-buried in sand and had to be searched for, dug up and collected. To pick them out, we had to scrabble on our knees and study the stones, feeling their weight and caressing their surfaces as only the sea had done before us.

A thin, dried crust of bladderwrack, empty shells, small gobs of caulking tar, frayed lengths of rope and bits of driftwood gave away the high tide mark. From there to the waterline was the best hunting ground: higher up the shore were the angular blocks torn from the hillocks beyond, while nearer the waves finer shingle was deposited. In-between, skimmers of the right radius were pressed by the retreating tide into shallow scrapes in the damp sand. We brushed them smooth of grains and filled our pockets. When looking up with the tang of salt heavy on our tongues and dirt under our nails, we discovered our vague anxieties about the place we found ourselves in had disappeared. We saw the terrain through different eyes.

The geology of the landscape began to reveal its

secrets, or perhaps it is closer to the truth that for the first time that day we began to listen to it. We were framed by hills that had rolled beneath the tread of terrible lizards. The smooth grey skimming stones in our hands had been frozen in ice-gripped tundra when Scotland was first formed and sculpted by countless glaciers and the erosion of the sea.

Taking it in turns, we started counting the skips aloud, both adding a phantom point to the tally when the other wasn't looking. With shouts of 'watch and learn', we aimed to pip the high score, which had reached a respectable 17 fairly quickly, but broke down laughing every time an attempt went unceremoniously wrong.

The autumn sun carried on its steady arc westward towards the horizon. Neither of us had seen the waters around Great Britain looking more impressive. The sea rippled like silk from our skimmers and we stayed at the waterline until darkness fell. Climbing into a tent lit only by the canopy of stars we felt something of the unity that John Steinbeck describes: 'One thing is all things – plankton, a shimmering phosphorescence on the sea and the spinning planets and an expanding universe, all bound together by the elastic string of time. It is advisable to look from the tide pool to the stars and then back to the tide pool again.'

The following morning broke brightly with birdsong. A beach that we had initially been 'trapped' on now displayed a very different aspect. By passing time in this place we were sharing in some of its nature. It had left its mark on us, like ripples from our stones merging into oncoming waves. We both took a good skimmer with us as we continued to Inverie, not so much a memento as a promise to ourselves to experience this again as soon as the opportunity presented itself. And we didn't have to wait for long.

Skimming stones around the peninsula's breathtaking coast we learnt that it is not just the relationship with the landscape that develops through a slowing of pace and an active engagement with the surroundings. As you search the shore for shapely stones, nestled down where the swell throws foamy fingers across great humps of seaweed-covered rock, there are exciting discoveries to be made. This area of not-quite-sea, not-quite-land is an environment for creatures that need to remain submerged, but which may be too fragile to survive the battering of the waves or the vastness of the sea itself.

These are pools filled with life. Looking into them, the eyes adjust to reveal a world brimming with exotic-looking flora and fauna. Sea anemones are deceptive predators whose bright floral appearance belies a multitude of infinitesimal harpoons lethal to small fish and shrimp. They dance above olive-green shore crabs scampering between cracks and crevices or digging among the sand for dinner. Charles Darwin hazarded that all life may even have begun here, 'in some warm little pond, with all sorts of ammonia and phosphoric salts', and some more recent scientists have lent support to this theory. Eons ago a rich broth of salt water and minerals could have formed where the land meets the sea and, heated by the sun, burst into life. Trudging across the irregular rocks, avoiding the bright, slick green of edible sea lettuce and forests of untamed gutweed, it's not difficult to imagine you have somehow crossed through a portal, back to the earth of millions of years ago.

Some of us will be able to recall excursions with net and bucket, picking our way across the treacherous rocks on a quest to capture monsters of the deep. Fascination with the alien leads us to risk the pinch of the crab, or test the anemone's wavy appendages as they sway with some gentle current, feeling the combination of thrill and revulsion at their distinctive sticky texture. The next moment our attention may be drawn to a faint sucking sound from a cliff face and, peering in, a thousand glittering eyes stare back. The goby at low tide clings tenaciously to rock crevices, in places only a couple of centimetres thick or less but cut deep into the strata. Even on the brightest afternoon, this is an unnerving crack into another universe, one packed tight with primordial creatures glistening in the darkness.

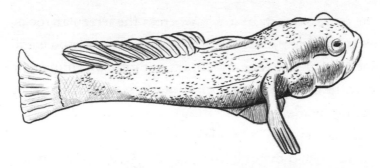

As adults, this connection may fade or be modified and muted by the knowledge that interfering is irresponsible, and indeed this is true: some fish and other creatures spend their entire lives returning to the same habitat with every tide, and are greatly troubled by being removed for observation. Limpets grow their shells and carve their spot on the underlying rock to make a seal; removing them in the open air is a death sentence. The size and position of a pool creates very specific variations in salinity and oxygenation over the course of each tide, and animals suited to one pool may die in another. Others pair with a partner, such as fish sharing a burrow with a shrimp in return for watching out for predators, and no one wants to split up a happy couple. Of course, the instinct to capture as much as possible served our ancestors well – the beach is a well-stocked larder all year round, and low barriers built up to form artificial pools could trap a good haul with every tide. But rather than the creatures themselves being the prey, our hunting instincts have been diverted to search for new experiences and sensations.

This is where the stone skimmer's joy lies. By joining

the other animals as a fellow user of a beach, by giving yourself a purpose, you allow nature to come to you. To the eyes of someone looking for stones, an empty pool may reveal itself as packed with stealthy swimmers hiding in plain sight. Shrimps and prawns are largely transparent with a subtle camouflage on their opaque portions, and their alternating stillness and speed makes them difficult to spot unless you take a few minutes to adjust. In the same way as some techniques of meditation intended to induce a higher state of consciousness start with intense focus on a single object, mantra or idea, concentrating on skimming stones does a wonderful thing. It helps expand your consciousness into the world around you.

Over time such observations can become more acute. We all recognise the squawking and screaming 'arc, arc, arc' of the herring gull, but watched in their natural habitat they reveal themselves to be feathered weathervanes. A stretch of shore lost under a congregating flock is a warning to the stone skimmer: 'when seagulls fly to land, a storm is at hand'. Because the gulls are unhappy resting on choppy waves further out to sea, you may be sure that harsh weather is likely to blow in soon. Spending time skimming helps develop a connection with the landscape akin to learning to read Chinese pictograms. Patterns begin to make sense.

In our experience, slowing the pace also gives animals a chance to grow accustomed to our presence. Few places instil a sense of natural rhythm more immediately than

Lindisfarne. We reached this 'island', located just off the north-east coast of England, via a causeway only revealed at low tide. From the outset, therefore, we were obliged to synchronise our bodies with the sea and elements. They respect no appointments in the diary but their own. As we crossed this temporary gateway on an October morning, the great mudflats on either side of the road bustled with waders: godwits, redshanks, oystercatchers and curlews in nattering congregation. The greatest surprise, however, came from a half-hour spent stone skimming on the south coast of the island. A silent visage emerged alongside the path of a twelve-bouncer. It was a seal looking on with all the attentive interest of a dog waiting for a stick to present itself. It blinked contentedly as others nosed their way up from the deep to join it. With their great, dark, liquid eyes, upturned snouts and expressive faces, seals are appealing creatures and three rolled on to the rocks some way off the shore, yawning and stretching. It was enchanting to be near such large wild animals so blissfully untroubled by our presence.

As the pups of the grey seal are born in autumn in the eastern Atlantic, this season is a rewarding time to be seal watching. The pups are initially baggy and shapeless, but soon barrel on fatty seal milk. They turn into sleek, silky snowballs of white fur for a month or so between September and November, before adopting the mottled waterproof coat of adulthood and setting out on their first fishing trips. The innocence and wordless expressions of affection between them remind us that the best things in life are free. It is not uncommon for a seal to take an entire day off from hunting in order to lounge with its colleagues. People too need to give up worrying about an uncertain future from time to time and enjoy what's here now.

We always believed that the best views of seals were only to be had through guile and cunning, quietly creeping over the crests of dunes with binoculars, yet here we were only 10 metres away, proving the chance benefits of spending time in nature are rich indeed. It is the pleasure of accidental discovery, like being surprised by a favourite song when tuning a tinny radio that somehow sounds different, better even, because it is unexpected.

Perhaps we all feel the need to set a target too strongly, marching across the great outdoors from A to B, projecting goals on to the landscape; to 'do' a long-distance path, to crest a difficult ridge, to set ourselves challenging time limits. Similarly, we are taught that there is much we have to pursue in life with every physical, mental or emotional reserve, just as a seal hurls its body through the water after a fish. Yet we invariably learn that many important things cannot be hunted into submission; beautiful and delicate, they will shut, shatter or shy away if we try to grasp them. Think of love.

Some of the earliest examples of human tools display markings that are functionally useless, testament to our need to pursue and display 'pointlessness' in all sorts of directions, games, art, sculpture, music and more. To harness the magical ability to turn an inert pebble into a tool of purpose and precision is to grasp something fundamental to mankind; it is to be transported to the dawn of human history itself, where taking pleasure in creation and experimentation led to our very evolution as a species. Of course, not every tool requires careful fashioning to become useful. Selecting a stone and giving it a purpose is among the most basic acts of creation, but it is satisfying in its own way. The embodiment of this principle is clear in stone skimming's universality and from the great range of cultures that indulge in it to this day.

With the possible exception of certain landlocked states, there is scarcely a place or race in the world that doesn't do it. Even in the frozen arctic, Inuit skim stones on ice, and in the deserts of Africa Bedouins have a version of the same game on sand. Records show that skimming stones was played in England as a sport in the seventeenth century, when it is said that James I would skim sovereigns across the River Thames in London. This is supposedly where the phrase 'ducks and drakes' came from; 'to make ducks and drakes' meant to squander your money foolishly and recklessly. But in our view it is more likely the game was named such because of the resemblance to the splashing contrail of waterfowl taking off. It is called 'skipping stones' or 'to dap' in America; 'skiffing' in Ireland, from the same root as the small flat-bottomed boat; and 'ricochet' in France. Most interestingly, the Danish call it 'smutting' and the Swedish 'kasta macka', roughly translated as 'to throw a sandwich'. To some at least, a good enough reason not to share your packed lunch with a Swede at the seaside.

Regardless of nationality, developing a skill like skimming stones, taking joy in its repetition and gradual perfecting, is a pleasure in itself. True, you may never trouble the world record (51 skims) or exceed the greatest distance covered (63 metres), but who cares? Is that even the point in the first place? Probably not. Stone skimming fits perfectly with that concept of ritual as defined by the author Evangelos Kyriakidis: 'a set activity that to the outsider seems irrational, non-contiguous, illogical even'. Yet, as in any ritual, it provides a permission, a doorway for us to enter a frame of mind that is displaced from everyday worries. We find ourselves standing in the midst of sheer life.

That stone skimming is the perfect passport into this other dimension, just alongside the ordinary, everyday one, shouldn't come as a big surprise. Similar use of stones to induce altered mental states permeates religious and spiritual ritual to this day. The archetypal shape of a skimming stone is almost identical to ancient Greek worry stones, used by monks on Mount Athos and still widely sold in health stores around the world. With an almost identical action to that of selecting a skimmer, people have for millennia held smooth, flat, round stones between index finger and thumb and rubbed them to lessen anxieties, regulate their breathing and to enter a relaxed, meditative mode of feeling and thought. Indeed, this rhythmic motion, a type of 'stim' or self-hypnosis, may even be the root of prayer beads in

Islam (called tespih), Buddhism (mala) and Catholicism (rosaries). Anyone who has spent a day collecting and caressing skimmers on a beach will certainly testify that the leap from skim to stim is not so great. Returning your concentration to the present moment, refocusing on a small object or a simple idea when your attention wanders, is related to the concept of 'mindfulness', allowing us to relax the usually continual processes of comparison, interpretation, prediction and projection going on in our heads.

As with prayer rituals, to skim stones and become absorbed in the moment is to cross into another world that exists all around us but cannot be visited or understood without being in the right state of mind. We're all born with an innate understanding of how to access it; we revel in it as children, but it is something so easily lost as we grow older. This is the essence of our experience writing this book: to follow a new set of rituals, taking the time to practise simple activities in the outdoors, is to become mentally present as well as physically located in the trees and forests, the fields and mountains, the rivers and seas that surround us. It is about learning the simple things that establish a sense of belonging in the natural landscape that many of us feel an innate yearning for. A vital connection is restored.

On the shores of Knoydart and Lindisfarne it was apparent how disconnected we can become. The terrain seemed a vivid, unfamiliar world to us, one that necessitated an adjusted gait to stride across stretches of sand, a listening to the unpredictable sounds of the sea, the inhalation of the distinctive scents and absorption into the distant horizon. We were impressed via every sense with novelty so far removed from the secure walls we construct for ourselves in the day-to-day; the regularity of the pavement, the air-conditioned office, the hum of the city, the endless false day of artificial light. This was tapping into another rhythm, one that we rarely glimpse in our modern city- and work-oriented lives.

Crucially, it gave us the space to reflect, and when skimming stones we felt a tangible calm descending over our bodies and minds. There was no real sense of what time it was, and it didn't matter. Like the stately limpets progressing around us at a gentle pace across the rocks of the high intertidal zone, their traces visible in the trails of algae on which they grazed, we had the time to experience nature's power, as expressed both in the endless rolling of the ocean and the far slower rolling of the landscape itself.

When the tide recedes, these maritime relatives of the snail hold the sea in miniature within their conical shells, shaped like tiny Chinese sedge hats, cementing themselves to the rocks until the water returns. Something as simple as skimming a stone can take on a great significance, leaving experiences that linger, tucked under our shell of memories, nourishing us throughout our lives.

Find a fossil

When you consider the awesome events they represent and the epic geological processes responsible for their creation, it seems odd that finding preserved prehistoric life can be as simple as rooting through loose stones at the seaside. But with a little patience and knowledge, that is all it takes.

The key is to search in an area of sedimentary rock that is regularly eroded by rough weather. This is rock that has been laid down in successive layers, and often displays a striped cross-section as a result. It is often softer than rock created by volcanoes or other processes. Beaches, foreshore and scree slopes found under crumbling coastal cliffs are the most bountiful and reliable examples.

Millions of years ago, these would have existed in a

different form. All sedimentary rock was silt, mud, sand or gravel eroded from even older mountains, or even the hard remains of organisms in the case of chalk. Washed down watercourses, they settled in layers on the bottom of prehistoric rivers, lakes and oceans, incarcerating many creatures, trapping the bodies of the living and the dead in an oxygen-free prison that prevented their natural decay. With the passage of time, extreme heat, pressure and chemical changes, these layers turned into stratified rock. Gravel became conglomerate, sand became sandstone, mud became shale and, locked within each, a myriad of organic matter became fossils. These are the focus of our search: shells, bones, petrified wood, footprints and leaves, everything from minuscule bacteria to giant dinosaurs that would have shaken the ground as they walked.

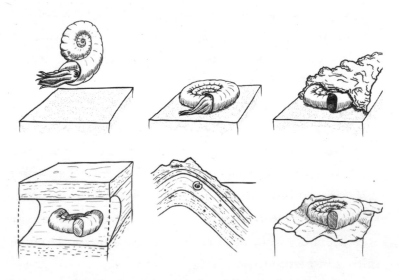

Although possible at any time of year, the harsh, wet winds and stormy seas of winter tend to dislodge more rock, and the process of freezing and thawing can crack even vast stone sheets into handy pieces, increasing your chances of uncovering something interesting. The added bonus of searching in this season is that you will most likely get the whole shore to yourself.

There are now many websites that detail fossil sites by period and give location information, which can be useful in choosing an area. Alternatively, you can chance your arm with an area of coast nearby. Either way, try to arrive just after high tide when the opportunity for discovery is at its greatest and the sea's return is many hours away.

Start at the water's edge and work your way back inland as though mowing a lawn. Draw an imaginary square that stretches from the waterline right up to the top of the shore. Slow your pace, lower your gaze and keep a sharp eye out, walking up and down the square methodically, sweeping your eyes from left to right in metre widths with each stride. This will ensure you cover the space thoroughly in a grid pattern.

A good fossil hunter should be able to tune in and subconsciously evaluate the ground they pass over quickly, a skill archaeologist Richard E. Leakey compared to 'a mental radar that works even when not concentrating hard'. This is particularly true when looking for fossils found near the tide line. Washed out from the cliffs or up from the seabed, they can litter the foreshore, becoming tangled in threads of seaweed. These are often the same colour as the sand in which they are found and broken down into smaller, odd-shaped fragments that blend almost perfectly with their background.

For less damaged specimens, sift through the shingle higher up your imaginary square particularly among the scree slopes that sit below the cliffs. Here caution must be taken, however. Many fossil finders wear hard hats for good reason, and if you are going to be spending time under any rock faces, make sure you are wearing one too. Around the larger rocks, look for areas where successive strata have been laid down. These may appear as 'steps' in a cliff face that alternate between large flat surfaces along bedding planes and wrinkled cross-sections, much like a giant '99 flake. Debris from these can prove to be a very rich source indeed.

If you are lucky, the action of weathering and erosion will have birthed a fossil for you, leaving little effort required to free it completely from its bonds. In fact, as a rule, it's rarely worth splitting a rock that doesn't already have a fossil visible; hacking into random bedrock seldom yields anything, and at the base of a cliff you are underneath, it is a particularly bad idea. Instead concentrate on looking for that partly exposed organic form. Then, when you do see something, take a moment to record its situation. A camera on a mobile phone is good enough, but it is also helpful to have some indicator of its size – a match, say, or a coin placed next to the fossil.

Keen hunters may invest in hardened hammers, chisels and safety goggles with which to tackle more stubbornly embedded specimens. Often as not, however, it is the back of the hammer that is most used in prising layers of rock apart. If improvising on the spur of the moment, a simple pocketknife with a sturdy blade will more than suffice.

By placing the tip of the knife or back of a hammer in the crack between bedding planes, it is relatively easy to lever two layers apart. Pry them open carefully to reveal the fossil, and then remove extraneous surrounding material or 'matrix' gently. As even the most intricate shapes of fossilised creatures have turned to stone over the eons, they will normally not come apart with the bedding rock, but over-zealous masonry can still shatter your find.

On most stretches of coast, collecting fossils like this is perfectly legal. Indeed, with the savage erosion of some of our shores, it is imperative we rescue rarer specimens from destruction. We must be respectful of the environment, however, and there are some exceptions, such as Sites of Special Scientific Interest (SSSIs), so check before you go.

If you are lucky enough to find something other than the more common shells and teeth, take note of your position on the shore and photograph the area. Surrounding rock can be helpful in establishing how old the creature is and greatly increase the scientific value of a find. Stumble on something particularly noteworthy, a whole skeleton perhaps, and you might consider informing a museum and letting an expert excavate your find. Many will give you a cast to keep, so you still get bragging rights, plus the satisfaction of contributing something potentially new to the scientific canon.

When you get home, it is a good idea to soak your finds in fresh water for at least a couple of weeks to remove potentially corrosive salts. However, submersing dry rocks suddenly can cause them to crack, so a good technique is to wrap them in damp paper towels for a few days to wet them initially.

Fossils bridge the gap between simple, almost mathematical shapes, and the infinite variation of the organic. This natural sculptural quality explains the collector's obsession: they are beautiful things to have on display. But as any fossil finder will tell you, as much enjoyment is drawn from the process of discovering them as from collecting them and, just as a single photograph can embody an entire holiday, a single ossified symbol can evoke many glorious hours spent searching at the seaside. The sense of achievement and wonder at uncovering even one alien imprint is an experience that is difficult to convey. You simply have to try it to understand.

On a freezing morning in early February we tried our luck on North Yorkshire's Jurassic coast, a stretch running up from the small fishing village of Robin Hood's Bay to Whitby. Emerging here is a 200-million-year-old strip of shale that England wears like a sash, sweeping down from its shoulder in Yorkshire through Humberside, the East Midlands, Gloucestershire, Somerset and out again at the Devon and Dorset coast.

A few miles over the snowy clifftop path, a

well-trodden slope broke away down towards the sea and, using the shivering stems of bramble and shrub to steady our ungainly slides, we clambered feet-first down the steep river gully until we hit the shore. We landed centre stage in an amphitheatre of epic proportions. Vast, bulging bellies of shale cliffs towered around us, their overhangs as though some cyclopean stonemason had hewed them into shape. Beyond the wide stretch of rock and sand, a grey-brown sea disappeared into a misty cloud of the same colour. Discerning a horizon was impossible. It seemed we had not only reached the end of the land, but the end of the earth itself.

The crunch of our boots on the wet pebbles broke the frozen calm as, hunching over, we began scanning for signs of once-living forms among the millions of dead stones, only looking up to check for the returning sea or when startled by cascades of loose mud and rubble that sporadically gushed in splattering crescendos from the cliffs above.

Any fossil finder will tell you that the hunting soon becomes an addiction. We both turned enviously whenever the other dropped to their knees and started scrabbling through the shingle on the trail for buried treasure, like prospectors in the California gold rush.

Soon enough we found it. A shard poked out slightly from the pebbles, dark blue-grey, about 9 or 10 centimetres in length and perfectly rounded like the side of a stick of rock. With some gentle persuasion we liberated the 'guard' part of a belemnite from the shale. The internal skeleton of an ancient squid-like creature, it tapered to a point at one end, finishing flat at the other. This has earned it the nickname of 'bullet stone', as the fragile 'phragmacone' and 'pro-ostracum' – head and tentacle sections – rarely survive. Sitting among the wet rocks, our numb fingers traced the shape of a something that had lived and died at least 65 million years before our own evolution. Here we were, the first to lay eyes on it, to touch it. The fossil is a great antidote to the detachment felt by a sophisticated urbanite. Although a very common find, to us it was as magical as if we'd liberated the Sword in the Stone.

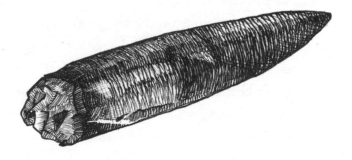

Spurred on, we started our search again and the next few hours seemed to pass in an instant. Rooting through the foreshore, our pockets were laden with sand-coated relics, each bringing us closer to a lost world. More pieces of bullet-shaped belemnite; fragments of 'devil's toenail', aptly named ancient oysters; and even a fossilised echinoid reminiscent of a miniature cannonball, that is distantly related to our starfish and sea cucumbers.

We were about to turn back and retrace our steps when we saw it, the most iconic example of these ancient organic shapes, a pure manifestation of the Fibonacci sequence. Underneath a layer of strata in the cliff, this beautiful, ribbed, snake-like coil rose from the edge of a foot-long slab of shale. The ammonite shell is the first thing most of us imagine when we think of a fossil and, as such, it was instantly recognisable. Named for the Egyptian god Ammon because of its likeness to his spiralling goat horns, ammonites have been found as large as 3 metres across, although this one was no bigger than the palm of a hand. Medieval Britons in the area took them for petrified snakes. They believed the fossils they found had been transformed by St Hilda of Whitby Abbey and, in true entrepreneurial spirit, carved a serpent's head into each before touting them to pilgrims.

After some experimentation, we mastered an approach to releasing our beautiful find, carefully chipping away with two bits of flint as a hammer and makeshift vice until its full form came away into our hands.

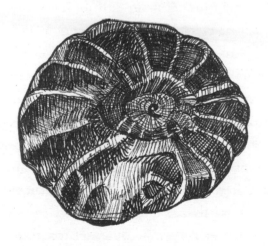

In modern society we are conditioned to always be working towards the next goal, and to demand instant gratification. Much like stargazing on a clear night, uncovering prehistoric life forces us to confront the awesomeness of time. But where stars can seem impersonal and outside our sphere of experience, holding the remains of a living thing is an immediate and powerful reminder of the precariousness of our own existence. The fossil is now just stone. It is not a living thing, it is not even the actual shell of a living thing. It forces us to engage with the reality of their total destruction. This is paradoxical; an excitement akin to discovering proof of life on a different planet coupled with a sobering reminder of the transitory nature of life on earth.

There is a past so distant it is tempting to write it off as irrelevant, but investigating what it has left provides a sense of perspective on the present. A shoreline is the product of processes that lie right at the edge of our ability to imagine time. Human culture has struggled with the concept of eternity in writing and thought since as far back as records go, and being confronted with the pattern of a dead creature preserved in stone creates in us a sensation that cannot be fully articulated. Catholic priest Father John MacEnery's 1825 account of finding fossilised life in Kent is filled with this sensation: 'As I laid my hand on them, relics of extinct races and an order of things which passed away with them, I shrank back involuntarily . . . I felt more of awe than joy.' Mundane materials have become elevated to products of magnificent artifice. They have the capacity to transform our consciousness.

The strata of a cliff face twist the passage of time into a cross-section, but there are also more recent layers of history to be found. Having scoured the area of shore on which we initially arrived, we traced the base of a scree slope around a promontory, and came upon a mess of twisted metal scattered all the way from the rocky beach into the water. There was no mistaking the broken hull of a wrecked ship, its remains rising like a clawed hand.

We discovered later that this was the *Admiral Von Trump*, a fishing trawler wrecked in 1976 in mysterious circumstances. But even without this knowledge, the haunting quality of any shipwreck reminds us that fossils are not the only records half buried in the fabric of the coast, nor the only remnants with the power to grasp the imagination. Nothing evokes the same sense of empathy with human history as a wreck. We can see and touch the harsh truth they represent. Like flicking through the pages of an adventure book, contemplating the fate of the 47,000 shipwrecks chronicled around our coast fills the mind's eye with images of the horrors people have faced in fierce battles with the mighty sea and with each other.

Sources dating back to the fourteenth century map the many victims of inclement weather, bad navigation and the long march of war down the centuries. A good number of these are just off our coasts in under 10 to 20 metres of water. They range from tall wooden ships smashed to pieces by storms to German U-boats like the *UC70* lying near the beach we were standing on, sunk with all hands almost one hundred years ago. We are used to having drama syndicated to our televsion screens from across the globe; we tend to forget the multitude of fascinating stories that lie, lost and submerged, only a stone's skim from our shores. Standing amid a wreck is a sure way to remind us.

Finding fossils encourages us to look more closely at the landscape around us. When we do, we often find that the most incredible discoveries can be made right here. Assuming we know everything about our surroundings and that there is nothing to be gained from taking the time to connect on a different level is foolish. Even the barest stretch of seaside may hold mysteries beyond our ken. Tuned in, when walking along a shore, you begin to contemplate what journeys things took to reach their resting places. Blocks of old concrete suddenly reveal themselves to be tumbledown pillboxes, and salt-rusted rivets the remnants of anti-aircraft gun emplacements. Among these, young soldiers once looked out to sea, no doubt wondering what form their futures would take with the threat of invasion looming. They remind us that one day we too will become history, the mighty structures of our age washing little by little into the sea. The tide was beginning to lap at our boots, and our bay of ingress was now cut off by the rising waves. We headed up partially collapsed wooden steps jutting from the steep clay of the nearest cliff face like the bones of some ancient leviathan. We emerged from the bare gorse bushes back into the modern world. It felt as though we'd travelled through time. There is a fundamental truth here: that we are all just passing through. Nothing is fixed, and as we made our way back to the electric lights of Robin Hood's Bay, we stood atop a vast history of life and death.

Fossils were, after all, the first time machines, greatly expanding the tale of the years we believed to have preceded us. They dispelled Archbishop Ussher's seventeenth-century assertion that our world began in 4004 BC, calculated by trawling the Bible and adding up the lifespan of everybody since Adam and Eve. Perhaps he would have been better off reading from the book of Job, 'Speak to the earth and it shall teach ye', for once humanity had entered into a dialogue with fossils, they pushed back the clock and lent weight to revolutionary ideas like Darwin's observations of the evolution of living species and Alfred Wegener's theories of continental drift. The theories of evolution and plate tectonics would subsequently necessitate revisions to vast swathes of human thought.

There can't be too many places left where, heading up some uneven stairs in a pub on a Friday night, you are confronted with a room of gusty singing. Those that do remain are keepers of a ritual that goes back hundreds of years at least, to a murky origin without written record. We chanced upon Ye Dolphin pub in Robin Hood's Bay, one such library of folk tradition, in search of nothing more than respite from biting winds that were numbing our fingers and reddening our noses. We were met with sticky faded carpets, salt-stained curtains, inexplicable side-rooms and unexpected staircases, and finally by a rotund, bearded man with a lyrics sheet who was ringmaster at this gathering. Peering over his crescent spectacles at the assembly, who ranged from 8 to 80, he led us in the chorus of a centuries-old sea shanty, 'Leave Her, Johnny, Leave Her'.

Remnants of the past like this can work on different levels. When you participate in their telling as we did, stories in song evoke characters and situations that feel as emotionally real as any film, play or book. Perhaps this is why such folk nights can be so brilliantly unself-conscious. Like a gospel congregation giving voice to a shared devotion, this was an outpouring of emotions otherwise held in check, a rite performed down the ages, founded on the rich seams of experience that still run through coastal communities. The themes are omnipresent: the struggle between birth and death, the drive to set out into the world balanced against the desire to return safely.

It struck us that folk songs, shipwrecks and fossils all have a similar effect; they establish a connection that is very different to television or other received media. You have to earn it by taking the time to participate.

Considering these shattered or crushed remains, or these echoing songs of days gone by, brings home the point that only certain hard structures withstand the tests of time. Creatures, cultures and ships pass by, leaving clues to their existence, powerful precisely because they are now gone from the world. Our picture of the prehistoric is made up of the hard-shelled creatures or the bones of larger animals – innumerable delicate forms have been lost for ever. Likewise, the catchiest shanties leave a lasting impression – surely everyone at least knows the start of 'Drunken Sailor' – and we find ourselves humming a refrain long after we have forgotten the verses again.

Once you have made the effort to attune yourself, you see that fossils are everywhere, not just in the graveyards of the coast, but in the buildings we live in. Traces of seabeds ripple through sandstone steps, and creatures reveal themselves in the marble slabs that line the atriums of offices. There is a poetry to the fact that when we create these institutions they are built to last, yet embedded in their very foundations are symbols that remind us of their impermanence.

There is another side to these things, best realised in a moment of reflection once the adventure of discovery is over and you sit in the warmth, thinking back on the day's activity. The creatures in your pocket are not living, the wrecked ships are gone from the economic ecosystem of the world, and while the songs of cannonade, forced separation, hardship, hope and homecoming resonate strongly still, they are from a time that has passed. Does this lessen their impact? Any fossil finder will tell you not. From this sense of temporal perspective, then, springs a draught that allows you to forget the transient demands of day-to-day life, to deal in a sanguine fashion with the challenges you face, and hold on to the things that really matter.

In our modern lives we continually have to adapt to change, to hold the stress of uncertainty in our guts and press on. How rarely we take the time to put that in perspective. Against the vastness that went before us, and the mortality to which we are all subject, any actions we take may seem insignificant. Far from meaning we should never strive to achieve anything, however, reflecting on this can remind us that our time on this planet is short. We should worry less about many of the concerns that fill our waking hours, and we should try to prioritise the priceless, the profound.

Perhaps we can all take heart from the example of an early fossil finder, Mary Anning. As a poor woman living in Victorian England, she was excluded from the male-dominated scientific community, despite unearthing the first ichthyosaur and plesiosaur skeletons, and many more besides. She lamented that, 'The world has used me so unkindly, I fear it has made me suspicious of everyone.' Yet she continued her dangerous work excavating under cliffs following winter avalanches and is now recognised as one of the most influential British scientists.

Most of us will leave nothing like this legacy, but if we are lucky then one day we will look back on our own lives across a seashore of consciousness littered with those memories that have come to define us, hardened into permanence, poised in the sand. There is a melancholy to all frozen remnants of the past, to hopes and dreams no longer held, near misses and moments of triumph long ago, but there is a joy too. Reflecting on these moments can be uplifting, their beauty concentrated by their transience. Like everything that has gone before, we will all eventually be another layer, a brief line in the ever-changing story of the universe.

Forage for food

The seaside and coastal terrain is nature's larder. With no poisonous berries or potentially fatal fungi, and much of what's on offer recognisable from the restaurant table, it is the best place for a forager to start. Gathering any wild food can be a daunting prospect and it is a good idea to begin with something that is easily identified and cannot be confused with anything else.

Mussels are one of our most common shellfish. Growing up to 70 millimetres in length, their shells range in colour from a brown-grey to a purple-black, with a pearlescent interior. Seeing these lying open and empty on beaches is a good sign that you are near a mussel-rich location. Although colonies will grow on the smallest patch of secure material, boat hulls, jetties and piers, these bivalve molluscs love nothing more than a stretch of rocky coast. Mussels too high up the beach often die of exposure in winter, while fish predate those permanently submerged and it is often too risky to try and reach them anyway. Head for beaches that have decent-sized outcrops of rock on the lower shore, submerged at high tide but fully exposed when the sea is out. This is the ideal zone.

Folklore suggests that mussels and other filter-feeding shellfish should only be collected in months with an 'R' in them, avoiding high summer when warmer, calmer waters may have increased bacteria levels. It is true that you should never pick anything where there is a high concentration of algae and especially not during a 'red tide' when potentially harmful algal blooms turn the seawater scarlet. However, seasonal conditions are less important than being well away from any human constructs, be it a house, harbour or town. Mussels sieve through gallons of whatever water surrounds them, including the effluence from sewage outlets or oil from boat engines. But if you harvest them responsibly and only pick from areas that are regularly and roughly washed by strong, clean tides, mussels can be eaten at any time. A good starting point may be to check websites for Blue Flag areas, where water quality is suitable for swimming.

The first sunny days of spring provide perfect conditions. The sea is chiller-cabinet cold and some of the other wild foods found on the seashore are at their best, notably the young, tender shoots of green vegetables emerging into the first warmth of the year. Aim to arrive on the shore an hour or so before low tide. Many websites provide regional tide tables and it is worth checking beforehand to work out your timings for the day. Twice a month, around the period of a new moon and a full moon, when the Sun, Moon and Earth form a line, a 'spring tide' occurs. This is not named after the season, but derives from the same linguistic root, meaning to burst forth and rise. Spring tides result in higher and lower waters than usual as well as stronger currents, revealing the freshest specimens.

Start by walking down towards the water, looking for any dark mass covering the rocks. Follow the tide as it retreats before working your way along and back inshore, keeping the encroaching sea a good distance behind you. Lift up seaweed and scour sea-facing rocks for the mussel's telltale wedge-shaped shell with identical hinged halves. These should be closed tightly if the mussel is healthy.

Mussels are usually discovered in vast colonies, stuck fast to rock faces or buried deep into crevasses, anchored by tough byssus thread. These 'beards' hold them securely through the roughest waves. It is easiest to harvest them with a pocketknife and a plastic bag; impromptu foragers can fill their pockets with enough for a decent meal, just twisting the mussel a few times and pulling free with a sharp tug. Gather shiny, unbroken and firmly closed specimens that are neither the biggest nor the smallest, but somewhere in between. Juveniles may not have developed a full flavour, while the bigger, older mussels can be too chewy; those around 40–55 millimetres are best. Don't be put off by barnacles, which sometimes cement themselves to the shell, but be sparing in your gathering and move a step or two after picking each one. This ensures a colony is unaffected and retains strength in numbers to face the battering of the sea. Estimate for half a kilo per person, around fifteen to twenty mussels each as a main course.

Once they are picked, hardier foragers might simply leave their haul in a bucket of fresh seawater for an hour, before placing them hinge down on to a layer of seaweed in the embers of a beach fire. Like a natural egg timer, mussels will helpfully demonstrate their readiness by opening after a few minutes, at which point a squeeze of lemon or some salt and pepper is all that is required to create a delicious seaside snack. Most would agree, however, that mussels are unrivalled when cooked in the French 'Marinière' style.

To prepare, first clean the mussels thoroughly by scrubbing with a stiff brush to remove any barnacles, sand or grit and tug away the remainder of their fibrous beards with your fingers by pulling sharply towards the hinge. Rinse and then let the mussels stand for an hour in fresh, cold, tap water, changing the water halfway through, before throwing away any that don't close when you tap them on the edge of the pan. Failure to close indicates the mussel is dead, and may therefore be rotten or diseased.

Soften three large shallots in plenty of butter in a large pan until golden and then add a generous slug of white wine. After another minute or so, add the mussels. Cover and let the steam cook them for seven minutes before removing the shellfish and stirring a little cream, pepper and salt into the remaining liquor. Pour this sauce back over the mussels in a large bowl, sprinkle with chopped parsley, and serve with crusty bread.

One mouthful and it's clear why a dish so simple to source and cook is rarely absent from the menus of expensive restaurants. Mussels are not only tasty, but good for us. Their subtle, meaty flesh is high in protein, low in fat and highly nutritious, rich in Vitamin B12, zinc, selenium, folic acid, iron, calcium, and omega-3 polyunsaturated fat, believed to be key in maintaining a healthy heart. There is a simple delight in their eating too. Served in a communal pot with diners using empty shells as pincers to pull out the meat or 'fish', they are the ultimate finger food. We enter a ritual of sharing that dates back to our earliest ancestors, seen clearly in prehistoric caches of discarded shells. Now, just as then, eating shellfish is a form of bonding as well as sustenance. Eyes meet, fingers touch, smiles are exchanged over who will take the last one. There is an intimacy that Roman writer Pliny the Elder may have overstated when he wrote: '. . . shellfish are the prime cause of the decline of morals and the adaptation of an extravagant lifestyle'.

The greatest pleasure, however, comes from sharing something plucked by your own hand from the wild. There is a story in its serving, one that adds a layer of appreciation. Most importantly, it instils the confidence to take that next step, to go out and discover more of nature's bounty. Once tasted, this freedom is empowering. It is accessible to rich and poor alike, and brings people together around a delicious meal. Liberté, égalité, fraternité through Moules Marinière.

The early March sun was hidden by cloud; a light drizzle mixed in the breeze with sea spray, a cooling atomiser. Shingle had been heaped into slippery banks by the tide and we waded down their flanks through pebbles still wet from the retreating sea. We had eaten wild mussels before, big blue-black beauties, plucked from the Atlantic and cooked over a driftwood fire, but that was in the wilderness of northern Scotland. Here, parked up just west of Dungeness, it took us a moment to adjust. Every service station we had passed had been the antithesis of foraging, stocked with produce from around the globe, packaged and sold alongside diesel and petrol. Food and fuel, treated with chemicals and dislocated from their places of origin, engineered to keep us going. Even driving through the rural backroads of Kent, a county christened 'The Garden of England', there were reminders of the distance we have come from wild food. 'Cherries', 'Strawberries', 'Asparagus': faded words chalked on to blackboards in lay-bys testament to the kind of intensive, high-yield fruits and vegetables that developed countries demand.

A few steps towards the sea and we felt the change. We were through the garden, out the back gate and down the path. Here, clusters of edible periwinkles bubbled from the rock. Despite the diminutive size (about 15–25 millimetres) of these dark, snail-like marine gastropods, they have been a vital food source for thousands of years and are still sold in many seaside towns, deliciously pickled in vinegar. Once boiled, periwinkles can be extricated with a pin in a process that spawned the epithet 'winkle picker' to mean a pointedly tapering toe on a shoe. Ironically, when eating from wild, you need to remove the winkle's own shoe, the hard 'operculum' disc at its foot, before popping it into your mouth. We lifted every fifth or sixth winkle, half-filling a plastic bag without making the slightest dent in their numbers. The only patch of mussels we found were too small to take. Dark, dense and wet, they lay at the base of a gully like splinters of broken glass.

With the sun brightening to the west, we followed it

along the coast and pulled the car over at any stretch of uninhabited rock or beach to continue the search. Near one sandy sweep, the waterline gave way to slabs of strangely angular mud; sharp ridges poked through the sand, remnants of root systems and branches. A sprawling, ancient forest had once filled the land where we stood. During its destruction, a snapshot had been preserved by salt water and mud, exposed by our every footstep. Wood and leaf litter lay in a dank black seam a few centimetres under the wet sand. Slicing through a waterlogged trunk, the edge of a small, folding spade met no more resistance than it would cutting a sponge cake. Thirty rings on a cross-section 6,000 years old.

Among this dead wood, living forests of dark greeny-brown bladderwrack were everywhere. In Chinese restaurants, many of us order crispy seaweed that is actually thinly shredded and deep-fried cabbage, but this was the real thing. A seaweed common on most shores, easy to spot and fantastic to eat, bladderwrack lives up to its name, ornamented with little blisters of air or 'vesicles'. These give buoyancy when the tide is in, lifting the fronds in the water to better draw in nutrients. They are also nature's bubble-wrap, and irresistible to pop, but the best bits to harvest are those lengths without either bladders or the squishy crab-claw-shaped tips, which perform the same function as flowers. When frying in oil, these tend to burst, sending showers of fat across the kitchen like gunshots.

Like most edible seaweeds, bladderwrack is stocked

with essential minerals and nutrients and is rich in beta-carotene and iodine. In the nineteenth century it was the original source of the latter and used extensively in diets to treat thyroid complaints like 'goitre'. To this day, iodine is just as highly valued in medicine and recognised as essential in the mental development of children. Worrying, then, that recent research suggests we get too little. One report found 70 per cent of young people tested in the UK to be suffering from an iodine deficiency. Yet the solution is all around us, and is best prepared by drying until crisp, deep-frying and sprinkling with a pinch of salt and sugar. We selected a bunch of the long, flat central fronds, knowing that after hanging for three days they would be perfect.

Advancing down the shore we came across the first outposts of a colony of mussels, raked by sunlight. Climbing down to their level, we saw they had commandeered the rock faces, wedged in their millions on a curving trajectory up and down the shore for as far as the eye could see. It looked as though lava had flowed down from the sandstone cliffs and stuck to the stone, cooled by the sea into a thick covering. Hurriedly we moved along their numbers, twisting and cutting. Our hands were wet, the sharp edges of the shells and the rough surfaces of rock stung our fingers, but we were reluctant to leave. Only when the crash of the waves licked our heels did we weave back around the headland, this time safely above the high-tide line. But this was far from the end of our foraging; we found instead that this was just a different aisle in the supermarket, one with a new abundance of delights on offer.

The first was an easy spot, a spiky green crown sprouted from the shingle bank. The succulent leaves were a rich, glossy green and looked like the young spinach we are used to buying as a salad leaf. Although plants can be more difficult to differentiate than the distinctive shellfish and seaweed we had already collected, we were confident this was sea beet. We double-checked online via our mobile phones before testing the theory. A small nibble at one of the fresher lower leaves proved the point beyond doubt. If anything, it was a sweeter taste than spinach, not bitter or salty as you might expect, and without that tendency to stick to your teeth. This was the abundant ancestor plant of beetroot, sugar beet and Swiss chard and we chewed its leaves raw, moving from mound to mound. We imagined the joy that early seashore-dwelling humans must have drawn from its emergence in the first days of spring. It was prized highly enough to be brought inland to grow as a crop, spawning the variants we use today.

Our next find sparked some debate. Sea kale is described in books on the subject as having fleshy blue-green leaves. What we had spotted was growing among shingle, crinkled and reminiscent of cabbage with tough wood-like stems lying half-swallowed by the gravel, but each burst of leaves was an unmistakable lurid purple. We reasoned that this was probably because it was young or dealing with specific environmental conditions. Many plants grow initially reddish leaves which then become green, or they produce the pigmentation to act as a natural sunscreen. The taste-test revealed a slightly bitter, peppery, but otherwise flavoursome shoot.

Young shoots of sea kale, also known as sea cabbage, used to be harvested in summer, having been intentionally buried under heaps of sand or shingle in the spring. A sprout half-buried by run-off from higher up the beach revealed why. The subterranean growth had lost all its chlorophyll and anthocyanin pigments, leaving it blanched white. A quick nibble revealed it had none of the bitterness of the stalks and leaves from above ground. It was one of the tastiest raw vegetables either of us has ever come across, akin to the white, crispy crunch of the heart of broccoli stems, but softer on the teeth.

The way to bring out the best in sea kale is well established. By the eighteenth century it was being eaten as a staple in many parts of the country. Records show it was served up to the Prince Regent in his pavilion in Brighton, while Mrs Beeton's famous 1861 *Household Management* describes it as part of a plain lunch for a 'middle class' family: 'Sunday: Clear gravy soup, roast haunch of mutton, sea kale, potatoes, rhubarb tart, custard in glasses.'

It was evening by the time we returned. We briefly boiled the few leaves we had picked, the colour changing from purple to an appetising deep green, before adding butter and crushed garlic, twisting in salt and pepper to serve. Alongside a pot of Moules Marinière, boiled winkles with a chilli dipping sauce on the side, and buttered sea beet turned with tagliatelle pasta and Parmesan, we enjoyed a seashore feast that enriched our minds as much as our tired bodies. A table of four was left fit to burst. What's more, it had cost us practically nothing. Such is the pleasure of foraging.

We live in a time when supermarkets rate among some of the biggest businesses in the world and are designed to account for every taste and dietary choice. We can order our food online and have it arrive without leaving the sofa. Cookery programmes have become primetime entertainment and we buy biblical-length recipe books on the culinary art. Rarely in our lifetimes will we find ourselves anything more than metres away from an available meal. Strange, then, that so many of us are so far removed from the reality of food.

There is now an increased awareness of the impact humans have on the ecosphere. This has manifested in moves to teach children about sustainable fishing, food miles and animal rights. While undoubtedly a positive development, it is an intellectual one, bringing us no closer to a personal, hands-on interaction with food and the natural world that provides it. A strong ethical compass may direct our buying choices, but we have lost the physical connection. We create a distance between the food on our forks and the mud of the fields. It is a necessary mental split if we are to keep consuming whatever lands on our plate without conscience, but it is ultimately dangerous.

Foraging provides an intervention; it makes us think

about food in different terms. Walking out on to the shore, we had to be certain of the things we picked, we had to know their descriptions and habitat, where to find them, how to harvest them sustainably, and at what time of year. Drawing closer to such details narrows the distance, creating a connection through seeing, touching, smelling and listening. We get to know the landscape through the identification and naming of its many parts, gradually becoming capable of differentiating between those plants and species we can and can't use. This intimacy deepens further still with selecting, preparing, cooking and tasting. Every speck of green on the upper shore becomes a potential find, every dark patch on a rock a possible mouthful. Small variations in the shape, texture or shade of a leaf signal the difference between merely palatable and positively scrumptious. There is a consciousness-shifting transformation, a new way of seeing and relating to the land around us.

This is not to suggest we should all abandon our weekly food shop and try to subsist on what we can find in the wild. It would be futile: our population is too dense and we would quickly destroy the landscape. Neither is it a call to return to the diet and living conditions of Cro-Magnon man, eschewing all wheat, sugar and modern crops, and fashioning all our tools from wood, flint and pieces of butchered animals. Technology enables us to be sure of the identity of what we gather, and devices we carry in our pockets can hold more lore than the wisest tribal elder. But it is rewarding to spend some time out in the elements, discovering what we can eat from the seashore. It gives us an insight into the mindset of our forefathers. We modify our choices based on what grows most abundantly and in the current season. Not only do we start to view the earth around us in a new light, we begin to recognise ourselves as a part of nature. Each breath is an interaction.

Grabbing the last bag of spinach in the supermarket, there is no way of being sure it isn't the last bag of spinach on earth. It is a naivety that marks how removed we have become from the origins of the things we eat; a destructive pattern that the author of *Charlotte's Web*, E. B. White, identified when he wrote 'I would feel more optimistic about a bright future for man if he spent less time proving that he can outwit nature and more time tasting her sweetness and respecting her seniority.' The technological mastery of crops is just such an outwitting, but it is important to recognise that, although it may one day cure world hunger, it has engendered a greater attitude of wastefulness in the Western world. We throw away colossal amounts of food as a society, much of which has never left its plastic packaging. Foraging for food can serve as a wake-up call. When we were gathering sea beet, the amount that was available on the stretch of coast was clearly visible. We picked it accordingly, only taking as much as we needed and leaving plenty behind.

Harvesting mussels and periwinkles came with another, more immediate consideration: the taking of life. We were selecting individual creatures that had lived for years on these particular rocks, while leaving others to survive. This may seem unnecessary, cruel even, when there is food aplenty nearby, yet every day those of us who eat meat unthinkingly sign the death warrants of millions of animals. We play God with these creatures, because we like the way they taste. But we do it out of sight and out of mind, at the supermarket checkout or in the rarefied atmosphere of a restaurant. How many of us could do the same if given a tool and a live beast? Probably very few. There is no gory mess when you kill a mussel, but having visited its habitat, removed it, and ended its life, you cannot help but have a more reverential sense of the value of food. It may seem contrary to our squeamish tendencies, but foraging helps us to appreciate what we eat more by re-establishing this connection. It brings a very real awareness and sense of responsibility, not only to take just what we need, but to hold what we have taken in high regard. There are implications to every bite.

In the distant past, wild food meant something very simple: survival. Today, few of us will ever be in the situation of having to rely on it to live. Instead, we found that foraging gives us a way to engage with the natural world in a positive fashion. It gives us a reason to be in the outdoors, to slow down and pay attention to the details. Like any Easter-egg hunt, it's not just the chocolate, but the anticipation and the triumph as well. There are great rewards from resurrecting a little wildness and intrigue. It has therapeutic value too, building our confidence to be self-sufficient and adding a new dimension to enjoying the countryside. We had only touched the surface on our trip – after all, there are books far bigger than this one filled with details on what you can find at the seashore – but we had learnt a new way of looking and it had stimulated an appetite to learn more about what is available in any terrain. The skill to recognise just a few staples brings a real feeling of power when out in the environment. We acquire the ability to unearth hidden abundance, to see things that were previously invisible. Banks of weeds become dandelion root coffee. Nondescript foliage reveals itself to be stocked with cough medicines, salad greens, medicinal teas. Walking with friends, we identify that oniony smell by a stream as wild garlic and pick the spear-shaped leaves as a delicious garnish for mashed potato.

Maybe it is this power that has caused foragers to be eyed with suspicion in the past. Those that drew their sustenance and medicines from the shoreline or the hedgerow were associated with scavenging and poverty, seen as uncouth and outside the civilised world. Their lore was an unwelcome reminder of a time when we were all wild, seeking nourishment, both physical and spiritual, in the plants and trees rather than the dining room and church. To some degree this attitude is changing. Top restaurants now sprinkle the adjective 'wild' liberally among dish descriptions to add an air of earthiness and as a synonym for stronger, more robust flavour. Most diners, however, would still balk at the idea of going out and harvesting it themselves. The declaration that you are going to forage for everyone's supper is more likely to be viewed with raised eyebrows than mounting excitement.

The irony is that most of us have picked blackberries without fear. We know when and where they grow, what they look like, and we even trust children to go out and identify their sweet, juicy fruits. We do this despite the fact that berries of the same colour found close by could be deadly nightshade, one of the most toxic and poisonous in the world. Our confidence comes from having the right knowledge, and foraging is simply a matter of expanding this understanding. In this sense, it is perhaps the easiest thing to do in this whole book, requiring nothing more than the time and commitment to look at nature in a slightly different way. When we do, we see how domesticated we have become; viewing the landscape and the animals and plants within it in two dimensions, demanding that vegetables have had the few remaining flecks of mud thoroughly washed from their surfaces. In the same way, we have washed the mud from our hands.

Facing an unwritten taboo like eating wild food, and finding it not just innocuous but delicious, is a nourishing experience. It is stepping through the frame and into the picture. Everything comes to life. When you feel the sea spray and hear the rush of the waves as you tuck into crunchy aromatic rock samphire picked from a cliff face, you are taking communion with nature. You cease to be a visitor. When you absorb the landscape it absorbs you too.

Make a kite

Most of us have felt the joy of sending a kite soaring at the seaside, but making one yourself takes the fun to new heights. The diamond kite is an iconic shape, and simple enough to build with materials lying around the house. All you need is two pieces of wood, a few metres of string, a bin bag and a roll of gaffer tape.

For the wood, thin dowelling or gardener's bamboo cane is best. Cut two pieces to measure 92 and 76 centimetres and lay the shorter 'cross-spar' over the longer one (helpfully called the 'longeron') 20 centimetres from the top to form a cross. Mark the join and use a pocket-knife to cut a small rectangle out of each cane where they meet so that they slot together, creating a stronger bond. This is easiest if you cut notches about a centimetre apart and remove the material in between by cutting sideways.

If you are using bamboo and a knife, you can lever the blade into one of the notches and the surface between should shear off, leaving the desired flat gap. Take care not to go beyond halfway through the thickness of the canes, however, as this will weaken them.

Bring the canes together and bind them tightly with string, making sure to wrap around the join in all directions and tie off the loose ends. This should be a resilient binding, springy enough to take some battering from the wind, but strong enough to hold the kite's form. Next, cut grooves at the four ends of the canes in such a way as to allow string to run around the edge of the cross in a diamond shape without slipping. Also cut two additional grooves into either end of the cross-spar, perpendicular to the first, so they resemble the top of a Phillips-head screw. Now you need to tension the cross-spar into a bow. Tie a piece of string to the longeron, just below the central join. Pull it to one end of the cross-spar and lay it over the horizontal groove. Bring it back along the other side of the kite, and slip it over the correlating groove at the other end. Pull this tight to bend the cane until it creates a 6-centimetre depth and then tie the loose end of the string to the longeron next to where you first attached it. This bow acts as a stabiliser that will help the kite right itself in the air. If the wind buffets it to the left, the left-hand side will face the wind more fully, naturally correcting the turn by rolling it to the right.

Now create the frame by threading the string around the outside edge. Again start by tying one end near the central join, this time on the cross-spar, then threading it straight up to the top vertex and looping it over the second, third and fourth cane ends and finally back over the first one again before tying. Keep enough tension that it does not come loose, but there is no need for this to be as taut as the string bowing the cross-spar. Once tied, use a blob of glue or sticky tape to cover each of the ends and prevent the various strings jumping out when the kite is airborne.

With the frame finished, lay the kite with the concave side upwards on a large plastic bin liner that has been opened out to form a single skin. Cut around it, leaving 7 centimetres clearance and fold each edge over the string, taping it into place. The sail does not have to be pulled taught. In fact, a bit of slack can help in flying. Imagine the tension of a plastic bag caught in a tree; the bag should cover the frame but not be stretched.

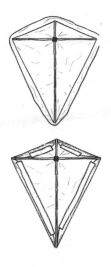

Now comes the most critical part of the process: adding a halter. Hold the kite in front of you and rest a finger under the central join to see which way the kite tips. A few pieces of extra tape on the lighter side should make it perfectly poised. Then make two pairs of small holes on the front of the sail, one pair almost at the nose and the other about 45

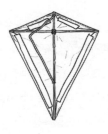

centimetres beneath the cross join. Thread a 100-centimetre piece of string through the front of the kite, round the longeron and back again. Tie it off and repeat with the other end through the other pair of holes. You should now have a halter about 90 centimetres long, accounting for the knots, that when lifted makes a triangular keel shape.

All that is left to do is to attach a running line of around 30 metres to the halter. Nylon string works well, especially if on a hollow tube that can be made into a spool by inserting a stick. Fixing this is best done when you are about to launch. The kite is easier to transport when free of its leash. When you are ready, tie the line on about a third of the halter's length from the nose. A simple noose in the halter at this point allows the running line to be tied with a slip-knot. This means the kite can be easily detached for adjustments or repairs.

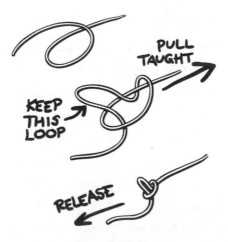

Kites can be flown anywhere there is enough wind, but the seaside offers some particular benefits. A strong offshore breeze is best; the sort British shores tend to excel at during mid-summer. The expanse of uninterrupted sea provides stronger and more consistent winds, with fewer up and down drafts, as well as an absence of trees and buildings that may curtail your aerobatics. On the right beach with the tide out, you are guaranteed a good launching spot and a wide, flat area to run about in.

Camber Sands in East Sussex seemed an appropriate place to launch our mission; its very name, meaning the slight curvature of a horizontal surface, brought to mind our curved aerofoil. The southern coast of England has long been famed for proud cliffs and bright beaches and the sun glinted off sand and distant sea in white and golden flashes. It was a picture postcard June day. Cresting the steep, soft, foot-sliding dunes, we could see the 6-kilometre sweep of flat sand was teeming with life. Dogs ran past sunbathers, horseback riders galloped along the waterline, and to the east were kite surfers, their vast canopies drifting lazily on the breeze.

In Britain, the prevailing wind mostly comes from the south-west, so a beach like this with an open southerly vista gives great lift. Even so, launching is much easier with a friend. Walking down to an open area, the gusts tried to seize our kite prematurely and we knew we'd found a good corridor for take-off. We designated launcher and flyer. The launcher faced into the wind, the flyer kept his back to it with about 10 metres of running line plus a little slack in between. Holding the kite above his head, the launcher waited, eyes shut against a raking of sand blown up by the breeze. The kite quivered like a horse in the starting blocks and was released upwards with a heave, both of us shouting with glee as it snaked its way into the atmosphere. Once airborne, it bucked and rolled like a Spitfire, making impossible turns in a dogfight. But after a few minutes, it spiralled down into the sand.

A carefully balanced kite will not need a tail, but they are improvised easily enough if the kite shows a tendency to rotate. We attached a couple of metres of string at the bottom and added ballast with strips of gaffer tape wrapped around it at intervals. This time it flew effortlessly. Soon we worked out that pulling the line accelerated the kite, while slackening provided manoeuvrability; keeping it soaring was about maintaining a steady medium, getting the feel right. With careful control, the darting diamond was staying airborne for longer. Ten minutes progressed to twenty.

What had been, only hours before, a lifeless assemblage of parts, now rose on to the breeze. We had transformed some sticks, string, a plastic bag and a plan into a triumph. This achievement was in stark contrast to the act of flying, where the enjoyment came not from meeting some goal but from the ongoing experience. As the kite danced across the flawless cobalt sky, we both found our consciousness following the slender path of string upwards to join it. The sand, the bathers, everything faded into the background and the sky was now where our attention sat. Author David Zanda knew when he wrote: 'I made you a kite so you would have to look up.'

We were somewhere else, high among the different layers that form in the atmosphere. Through the tension of the string between our fingers, each gust of wind was sent straight into our central nervous system, every thermal pulled us out of ourselves a bit more. Even when the prevailing wind and the sun's lazy arc brought the kite right in line with the eye of heaven, leaving us flying by sense of touch alone, the feeling did not falter. We were swimming in endless blue.

People spend years trying to achieve meditative states that allow them to feel an 'out-of-body' experience, but this was one kind that every child can attest to. Building and flying a kite goes deeper than feeling the wind on your face. It ties this wonder at the earth's natural power to another human instinct: the harnessing of the elements with our own hands. Despite huge, shop-bought kites being flown expertly nearby, parents were being dragged over the golden sands to watch us, Sussex's own version of the Wright Brothers. It was our glorified bin bag hovering and soaring like a bird that drew the gasps. The delight of the homemade is contagious and more than one toddler had their dads promising to make a kite when they got home.

It occurred to us that childlike fascination most likely launched the first kite. In one sense, building a kite is a fusion of art, science, aerodynamics and mathematics, but long before such disciplines existed, children with access to some form of thread and time to experiment were surely making flying machines. Nature is full of inspiring examples: helicopter seedpods, dried leaves and puffs of airborne dandelion, all wrapped up in a simple dance with the wind. If one of these were attached to a line, the smallest hand could control them.

The joy a child feels as they interact with the elements is captured in a story about Benjamin Franklin, American founding father, polymath and kite aficionado. Wishing to fly his kite, but not wanting to cease bathing in a lake on a warm day, it occurred to him that he could do both: 'He surrendered to the wind's power, lying on his back and letting the kite pull him clear across the pond without the least fatigue and with the greatest pleasure imaginable.' No doubt inspired by this kite surfing, Franklin went on to join the ranks of early weather scientists, suggesting that lightning was electrical in nature and that flying a kite into a thunderstorm and attracting a bolt could prove it. Mercifully, this was borne out by a less dangerous scientific procedure before he had the chance to try it.

Active imagination has long read the mighty forces of the natural world in a fantastical way. Lightning is Zeus hurling thunderbolts, the wind-blown waving of the treetops is down to wood nymphs and dryads; even Sir Arthur Conan Doyle believed faeries moved through the grass at the bottom of our gardens. A more scientific approach isn't any reason to lose this sense of wonder in a world that is constantly moving of its own volition. Indeed, much of the Western history of kites follows the pattern of creating an avatar to extend our limited human senses into a greater understanding of nature, sending something of and from us into the sky.

In 1749, Alexander Wilson and Thomas Melville tied thermometers to half a dozen paper kites to take temperature readings. Since then, kites have been used to carry progressively heavier payloads to progressively greater heights, literally and metaphorically. What plane can stay aloft as long or as cheaply as a kite? By the nineteenth century, this modern use for kites joined with more ancient knowledge flowing in from the east, where Chinese, Javanese, Japanese and Malaysian cultures had been making them for thousands of years. Attending Chicago's World Fair in 1893, *New York Times* accountant William Abner Eddy made a most notable connection. He was intrigued by the subtle differences between Malaysian kites and his own designs, and set about perfecting a stable and reliable kite that would become an icon: the Diamond Eddy. Eddy never thought to patent his ideas. Indeed he barely profited from them at all. All his rewards seemed to come from experimenting with his ideas.

The process of building something certainly makes it more meaningful. No shop-bought kite can give quite as much satisfaction. The night before our success on Camber Sands, we had cleared dinner off the kitchen table and set to constructing. Different members of the family we were staying with became intrigued, stopping to discuss how taut to make the bow or suggesting another type of knot. There is craft in the making of a machine, a bond that has tied fathers and sons for generations, but one that is perhaps being lost. Once flown, there is a bond with the kite too and an urge to reward it with decoration, to draw it closer to the birds it mimics. Packing away your avatar at the end of the day can leave a curious sensation. The kite has become bird and, like the screeching German owl 'kauz' that gave the machine its name, there is a sense that it should be let free to continue its journey – as if, without the wind in its sails, its spirit has gone.

This kind of anthropomorphising has been shown to be important in children's development, helping them identify with nature, making them more attuned, confident and imaginative. It has been vital to human progress as well. As late as the eighteenth century naturalists in developed countries argued as to whether birds migrated, but for thousands of years more 'primitive' civilisations had known it to be so. How else would Pacific Islanders have worked out they could cross the seas than by watching migrating land birds flying the same patterns year after year? With their early mastery of sails, perhaps a kite flown among them was another step to relating to these birds and understanding the winds better, giving them the confidence to cross seemingly impossible distances over the vast ocean.

Kite flying is a simple way to reach out towards the birds, towards the air above us, and to the clouds that sail across it. Keats knew it: 'To one who has been long in city pent, 'Tis very sweet to look into the fair and open face of heaven, to breathe a prayer, full in the smile of the blue firmament.' Looking for images in the puffballs and brushstrokes of white and grey stimulates our imagination. The expansive horizon at the coast provides an opportunity rivalled only by the highest mountains to gaze upon the families of clouds from the humble cumulus less than 1,800 metres above us, to lofty cirrus more than 5,000 metres above.

Lost in that other realm, we were surprised at how far we had travelled down the beach. Surfing thermals had led us in a criss-cross pattern towards the sea while our bags were ensconced in scrubby dunes a kilometre back along the shore. But having just spent such an uplifting few hours, we walked back across the compacted sand with beaming grins. We revelled in the great stretch before us just as the kite had allowed us to revel in the vaulted dome above. Coming back down to earth gave a giddy elation at the synergy between our creation and the raw power of nature.

The benefit of a sandy beach is that this synergy can take other simple forms. All around, others were busy echoing the work of early Britons trying to create the most elaborate and effective lines of defence against a mighty invading force: building sandcastles. From filling and upending a bucket on the sand to surrounding central keeps with smaller fortresses, protecting all with outer walls and moats, such is our obsession with forming ever more elaborate constructions, researchers from Bournemouth University have taken the time to determine that one part water to eight parts sand gives the soundest structure! Drier grains of top sand will not bind together and anything below the water table becomes liquefied, but a mix of the two works perfectly.

Some people prefer other games: a spot of beach boules or acrobatically keeping a ball aloft with enlarged ping-pong paddles. Regardless, a sense of play is important to us, whatever our age. Sandcastles, making kites, beachcombing, all involve creativity and imagination: they put you in charge. Sandy beaches in particular are more encouraging of games and evocative of high summer. We want to run and play on them. Sand is one of the few perfectly flat formations in nature that is easily moved and shaped. With the right sea currents, it is a runway, pitch or plot as pristine as any testing track, sports ground or building site. Whether we want to make our mark on it, or make good use of it, we can do so safe in the knowledge that it will be wiped clean and ready to use again the next day.

Most evocative of age-old tradition is family or friends setting up stumps, three dark lines matched by counterparts etched in shadow. Cricket has been played since at least the sixteenth century, and probably much longer, and has moved from village pastime to the second most popular sport in the world. The beach version is more forgiving of a wide range of ages, sizes and abilities than many other sports. Sand is a great leveller in more ways than one, reducing the advantage of fast runners, and giving rise to all sorts of random bounces that may scupper even the best aim.

We watched with the sun behind us as a family measured out a wicket. The game progressed with all the usual elements: an overly cunning bowler repeatedly failing to get any spin on the ball in the sand, the fiercest-looking batsman being dispatched by a small child, and the destruction of a nearby sandcastle in a spectacular dive. We left the beach carrying our kite and they were still going, their long shadows stretching towards the water.

It is in the nature of play that it has to end eventually.

The moments of success during the process of flying are what is valuable. There is no 'final' success with a kite. It must always come down. But the mood it engenders stays with you; our simple tethered sail had led us up to the gods of the sky. It had brought a flood of sensory information to its operators. Focusing so completely on it raised a philosophical question: where does a person end and the outside world begin? Ultimately, everything is made of the same particles. Hair blown in the wind is not alive, but because it was created by our bodies and is attached to our heads we feel it is part of us. Flying a kite you've built yourself is not so different.

You may say that a kite is not part of us because we feel no pain through it, but it *is* almost painful seeing something you've laboured over so carefully slam into the sand. Just as a motorist in an accident will use language that suggests they have become the car – hey, he just hit me! – we project awareness along the twine into the avatar, forgetting the grounded self. Conversely, people who suffer in an accident sometimes display an ability to distance their minds from their bodies, retreating into the safety of thought as a coping mechanism. We can go outwards and inwards.

When the first early human struck the first shard from a flint, had he or she planned it through some abstract thought process or was it an accidental act, one that then became part of a new way of thinking about the world? Surely the latter is more likely, and it raises an important truth: cognitive processes are not separate from the material world. The physical objects in a room or the places we go become part of our thinking. Cambridge neuroscientist Lambros Malafouris is one of those who suggests that the commonsense view of mind and body as separate, and our view of the brain as wholly containing the mind, could be fundamentally wrong. Rather, our bodies and our tools are part of our minds. When you are working out a complex sum you write numbers down, these are part of the mind's process, but outside the brain. Without the piece of paper, it is much harder to think through the problem. Think of a blind man and his white stick: removing the tool changes his mind's view of the world. If this is true, then adding a tool could result in the opposite: expanding our ability to think. The body, and the body extended by tools or location, is as much part of our minds as our brains are a part of our bodies. Some of us already know this intuitively; simply being able to take a stroll can be a vital component of a creative process. Wordsworth composed his poems walking in the outdoors. To what new pinnacles of thought could a kite lead? Alongside the childlike wonder and joy, there is a very real cognitive benefit – it expands the mind.

Importantly, you cannot expand your mind simply by imagining what it would be like to fly a kite, or reflecting on memories from your youth. You have to actually fly a kite, because then it is not wholly under your control. At times you must wrestle for influence, while at others the air and your aim become one. This is the beauty and fascination of nature: 'e pur si muove', Galileo said, 'and yet, it moves' – from stars to planets to the spheres of air, all is moving according to its own nature. Our will can only shape it so far. Sometimes you have to go with the flow.

Perhaps it is merely their height, but children seem to spend a lot of their time looking up, imagining shapes and possibilities in the clouds. As adults we are more concerned with looking down, on maps and via satellites whizzing overhead, delineating areas of responsibility and ownership. Playing with a homemade kite, experiencing the freedom of the coastal and the aerial 'terrain' on a summer's day, should be something we all revel in more often.

Fields and Forests

Carve an elder whistle

Making an elder whistle involves making a few cuts into the right piece of wood. Quick to execute, it only really requires the most minimal of woodworking equipment: a pocketknife.

Elder is easy to identify at any time of the year. It reaches a maximum height of about 10 metres and, when in leaf, has a bushy-green, shrubby look. Closer up, the leaves are oval shaped, finely serrated around the edges, and always grow on the stem in opposite pairs. In spring it has clutches of green buds that bloom into masses of heavily scented white flowers during early summer. By autumn these have given way to rich, dark-purple berries drooping down in thick clusters. Look for its distinctive bark, which has a cracked, corky and criss-crossed appearance and is creamy-brown or grey in colour.

Squashy pith, which makes it such an ideal whistle-making material, runs through the core of the wood. Inspect fallen branches or snapped twigs for this soft, circular heart, very different to the encasing wood; it is easy to hollow out and yields to a fingernail much like the polystyrene packaging used in parcels.

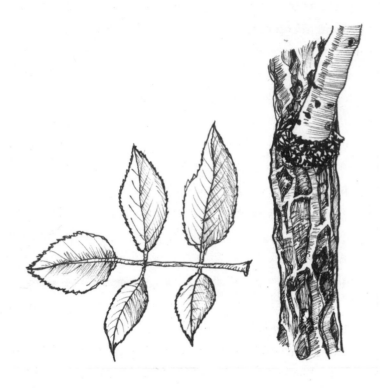

Growing prolifically in woodland, gardens and hedgerows, you are also likely to find elder at the margins of fields and forests around disturbed earth sites like rabbit warrens where churned ground and droppings provide a ready source of nitrogen. The tree's hardiness, versatility and preference for poorer soil means it is also a coloniser of towns and cities, and is found around roadside verges, parks, wastelands and railway lines. The ongoing maintenance of foliage in such areas means great banks of it are often cut back and dumped, providing ripe and ready pickings for the eagle-eyed whistle maker. Wherever you source the elder, however, it is best to carve it in woodland; a natural workshop is a far more stimulating environment to create.

Start with a straight branch just a bit thicker than your index finger and 9 or 10 centimetres in length. At this width it will be around two years old and the pith inside should be at its widest, taking up most of the cross-section. The pith to wood ratio is important; the tube needs to be hollow enough to create a decent sound chamber, but not so thin that it splits during the whistle's creation. Ideally the encircling casing will be 2 or 3 millimetres thick.

Shave away the bark with a knife until you reach the smooth, ivory-white wood. Then, with a small stick, push out the pith in the middle and scrape around the inside to leave a clear, wooden tube. Next, make a 'voicing mouth' about 2 centimetres in from the end you intend to blow into. This is a notch with one straight edge (closest to the end), and a rounded opening below that points down the length of the tube and resembles a smile in the wood. Cut it by slicing vertically down at 90° and then meeting this line with a 45° cut. Repeat until the sound hole spans almost the width of the whistle, revealing the hollow space within.

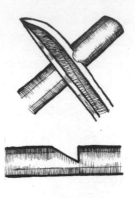

Now comes the mouthpiece. Find a round stick that is a touch wider than the end of the whistle. Don't use elder. Rather, snap off branches of any other type of tree. Use dead sticks as green wood will shrink, dry out and change the whistle's sound. Strip away the outer bark, but maintain the branch's roundness and keep testing the fit of the dowel by pushing it into the end of the whistle, making small adjustments with your knife. Leave the stick long and you'll have plenty of room for error and you can always trim off any mistakes and start again. It can be tricky to get right on a first attempt, but the fit of this 'fipple plug' has to be snug and airtight and completely fill the 2-centimetre space between the sound hole and the end of the whistle.

When the dowel is the correct thickness and length, cut a slice off it with one or two decisive strokes. In cross-section, it should look as if the top fifth of the circle has been removed. This surface allows the air to blow along it and hit the voicing mouth cleanly, whereupon it splits the flow to produce the whistle noise.

Fit the dowel into position with the flat top aligned with the voicing mouth. Cover the other end with the tip of your finger and blow into the mouthpiece. If it doesn't sound, you may need to make adjustments, clear the airway or remake the mouthpiece, but if the fit is good, a clear note will emerge. You can now fit an airtight dowel at the other end to seal it and decorate it as you wish. Whether crafted with a use in mind, for calling a dog perhaps, or as a rudimentary instrument, carrying a homemade whistle is an empowering feeling. You have turned the wood to your purpose, combining knowledge and skill to create something that resounds in us far longer than the note carries in the air.

The long days of summer were shortening when we first made whistles. The little wood felt rich and drowsy, nutty-scented and thick with the tawny light of afternoon. It was late September and the trees were shaking out their finery, a succession of bright, warm days and cooler evenings had trapped sugars in their leaves and the green chlorophyll was changing into ambers and reds now painted across the papery canopies. It was a glorious day.

We found a fully kitted glade and slung our rucksacks. Spotlights of sun fell through the trees overhead to light our workshop tables of sawn tree stumps and free refreshments abounded in the bramble canteens, blackberries mellowing and ripening in the ochre glow. Beyond the trees lay a vista of rolling yellow wheat fields; harvested two months earlier, they were trimmed into a drastic, stubbly crew cut. We had already obtained our key material by the field boundary, from an elder that seemed burdened by its fruit, bowed and bent, almost willing us to cut away a branch to ease its load. One was enough. Now, seated under an oak tree, we sawed it into two pieces and set to stripping away the bark, our knives exposing the blonde wood with each shaving. Each stroke birthed another twisting curl of soft green cambium layer, which gave way under the blades like butter. It was wonderful work, the smell of the inner bark a dense, leafy brew, perfuming the air.

Carving is one of the most therapeutic pastimes. It is understandable why rehabilitation workshops treating people with trauma or physical injury will often use the process of reshaping and reordering wood; it is psychotherapy and physiotherapy, pulling us out of the everyday routines with a gentle focus. Tracing the minutiae of the grain, our minds immediately switch to the small scale and become entranced; our hands busy in the process of creating order. There is no room to think of anything else. Each sweep of the blade changes the form and has to be carefully considered; we take part in a living, evolving process that roots us completely, also ordering our thoughts unconsciously as we work.

This level of concentration had rendered our whistle making surprisingly silent labour, yet the woodland was far from still. The industry of the autumn rang out in noisy contrast to our quietness. Unseen birds fluttered through the undergrowth and grey squirrels squeaked, scratched and squabbled about trunks and branches, competing for territory and beech mast, acorns and hazelnuts to fill their winter stores. Occasionally a crow flapped out of the trees in a shocking squawk. The dutiful labours of nature were simultaneously an inspiration and a distraction as, with every burst of noise or chatter, we couldn't help but peer around for a source. Sitting there, working in the midst of a vast forest factory, we were quickly subsumed; just another cog in the wheel, but, as such, part of a wider community too, one that stretches beyond the human.

Part of the thrill of woodland is the stark relief it gives us from the everyday, a non-human otherness that comes from being in nature. Watching any animal, even one so common as the grey squirrel, reminds us of the mind-bogglingly varied contemporaries we share our planet with. Our day-to-day struggles and demands encourage an egotism that renders us inwardly focused. Yet there is a simple thrill in observing the existence of other creatures, a reward in taking time to contemplate characters so alien in many respects, and so like our own personalities in others. Autumn in a wood is one of the best times to watch as nature busies itself for the cold of coming winter. We found ourselves in the midst of a looting frenzy. It was like the January sales on Oxford Street and, as we sat traffic-island-like in this leaf-strewn woodland road, mammals, insects and birds zipped around, and occasionally over us with their miniature mandibles, cheeks, paws and beaks brimming with bounty.

The bargains proffered by the terrain at this time of year aren't merely for the animals. Often by just stretching out a hand, the whistle maker may follow the example of the squirrels, liberating early sweet chestnuts from their spine-coated cases to roast later in the embers of a fire. Other hoards lay close by us too, early sloes for gin on blackthorn bushes, rowan berries for jams, even a mound of dark eyes peering from crocodilian lids – the split green husks of horse chestnuts. Unlike their sweet namesakes, these aren't edible or, indeed, any good for horses. But they have another use. Prepared according to arcane and often closely guarded rituals involving anything from saturation in vinegar to being half-baked in an oven, the horse chestnut makes a crude but effective weapon. Drilled and attached to a length of string, it has been used in playground battles for centuries and, to this day, conker contests remain knight-like in their chivalry. Alternate turns are taken where the aim is to hit the opponent's conker with your own. Even if you miss with your attempt, you must still stand and prepare to take the punishment. The loser is the conker bludgeoned to pieces first, the victor tying a knot in their string to signify the scalp.

Horse chestnuts are compellingly tactile forms to hold; dark, woody and cold, polished like miniature charms to be sequestered in a pocket and dug out unexpectedly at some later date. They are wooden eyes that bring a vision of childhood battles past. In 1917, for one autumn at least, they were being collected for far more lethal skirmishes. The British government enlisted schoolchildren to gather and donate conkers for use on the Western Front. We can only imagine what strange weapons children thought the Ministry of Munitions would be employing against the Germans, but in actuality horse chestnuts had been discovered to be a vital ingredient in the production of cordite for explosives in shells. The whole operation was conducted under a veil of secrecy and it led to many bemused enquiries from locals up and down the country as to why mounds of decaying conkers had started to appear beside railway stations. It seems ironic now, given that scientists believe they may prove to be a green energy source of the future. If this bears out, it is only fitting. Wood has provided our fuel and building materials, our toys and instruments for millennia.

Expelling the last of the pith from our wooden tubes with sharp breaths brought to mind another use for elder's hollow quality: the rudimentary blowpipe or paintball gun. The term 'elder-gun' appeared in dictionaries of the nineteenth century, referring to a popular homemade launcher for elderberries easily constructed from a 30-centimetre length of hollowed branch, and a slightly shorter plunger of hazel or a similar wood. The plunger was made to form a rough seal by pulverising and wetting the end so it splayed out. Pushing a berry into the midpoint, and placing another at the back, the aim was to slam the plunger into the tube, building up the air pressure until the foremost fruit fired forth with a 'pop' and struck a target to leave a miniature purple bloodstain.

Maybe it says something about the human condition or, at any rate, the need to exert control felt by young children, that we so readily turn to making weaponry. From an early age, the woods are perfect armouries for little hands, providing a place to make bows and arrows, elder blowpipes or catapults from a 'Y'-shaped stick. Even a boy with the most expensive plastic rifle in his toy box will derive as much pleasure using his imagination to turn a simple piece of bent wood into an improvised machine-gun. Stalking through trees in some imagined drama, the mould of the grip and the straightness of the barrel feel so real that a favourite branch might be carried home at the end of the day, only turning back into wood when stepping through the front door. As we get older, we lose this absorption, this personal connection with *a* tree or *a* branch. The projection of ourselves on to and into wood ends up like much of our imagination and creativity, diverted into the world of work or wearied from the effort of carving a place in society. Many of us slip unknowingly into a state where we can't see the trees for the wood. The forest becomes an unfamiliar place, an amorphous mass fringing the road or over the fence. The varieties of trees, each rich with their own personalities and traits, get lost, little more than a blur on the edge of our vision. Something as simple as carving an elder whistle brings us back. Re-establishing this relationship, turning wood to a purpose, channels our creativity again and fills us with a sense of control. As adults, when we scrape under the bark of any tree, we discover stories that run deeper than it would have been possible to imagine as children, often to the very heart of our history and language.

The word 'elder' is thought by some to have originated from its hollowness, a derivation of the Anglo-Saxon word for fire, 'æld'; the pith made useful tinder and the stems pipes to blow air that encouraged flames. In Scotland, it is still called the bour or bore tree, stemming from the Old English word *borian*, meaning 'to hollow out'. Others suggest the name comes from the ancient Danish, German and English myths of 'Hylde-Moer', the Elder Mother and guardian of the tree. This would certainly explain elder's long-held association with witchcraft, and as late as the twentieth century it was custom for some country folk to ask the 'Old Lady' for permission before cutting her branches: 'Old girl, give me some of thy wood and I will give thee some of mine when I grow into a tree'. Such rituals have been widespread around the globe for thousands of years, perpetuated by stories like that of a woodsman who cut an elder and watched it bleed, only to pass a witch as he returned home and notice, to his horror, that she bore a bloodied bandage on her arm.

The superstition undoubtedly has roots in elder's very real powers. There is natural insect repellent in its leaves, which would have seen them broken and rubbed on skin to stave off biting insects. Branches would have been tied on horses' bridles and left outside dairies, barns and privies to ward off flies, perhaps leading to the belief that it also offered protection against evil spirits. Maybe the notion of its potency grew from its efficacy as a cure. Elder has long been put to use in medicine, the scented flowers and berries made into delicious cordials, tisanes, wines and beer. In 1644, a book was published entirely dedicated to it: *The Anatomie of the Elder* by Dr Martin Blockwich. Pliny, an 'elder' himself, recorded the Romans treating a range of illnesses with the tree's fruits and, during the First World War, Maud Grieve wrote pamphlets instructing on how to prepare it to offset the paucity of conventional medical supplies.

Concoctions made from its flowers and fruits are still widely believed to be effective blood purifiers and anti-virals and remain a key product in healthfood shops and natural medicine. Indeed, tests in conventional science have shown certain extracts to be effective diabetes medicine and help reduce the symptoms of influenza. Certainly, the flowers make a delightful and easy tea when gathered in spring, slowly dried in the sun or an oven, and added to boiling water. They can be stored for the colder months in airtight jars and each time you open the lid, the smell is like spring itself coming to life.

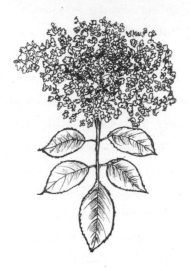

In common with other trees with white blossom, such as hawthorn and rowan, the elder has long been thought to be the favourite dwelling place of faeries, said to love the music from flutes, panpipes and whistles made of this wood above all others. As we put our newly fashioned instruments to our lips, we wondered what strange creatures might be drawn to our glade.

Two sylvan notes rang out across the clearing and echoed together through the trees. One deemed to carry higher, the other hanging among the roots, before both were eventually absorbed back into the wood that had created them. We found out later that, quite by chance, we had made a G♭ and B♭, the notes determined by the randomly chosen length of the sound chamber; the smaller you make it, the higher the pitch. We blew them again, surprised that they resonated together so beautifully, but intrigued more that they had caused no disturbance. An elder whistle produces an organic, woody note, throaty and warm, closer to that of a bird than anything else. No animals disappeared. This was unexpected and contrary to how we as humans think of the continuous note, used historically to marshal and direct. To us, it remains a strong signifier of First World War trenches, the police or football referees. We sent another beautiful harmony into the autumn breeze; it was as though we had found the language of the forest itself.

An aspen tree somewhere picked up the hint. Its leaves rustled like a crescendo of cymbals. Cocooned in the russet clearing, we could appreciate what Keats said of this season, 'thou hast thy music too . . . Hedge-crickets sing, and now with treble soft the redbreast whistles from a garden-croft; and gathering swallows twitter in the skies.' When you think about it, much of the pleasure of nature is musical, and this certainly becomes more apparent to an ear that has spent a day listening to nothing else. Assured of the clarity and quality of our instruments, we carved lip indents into the mouthpieces so that they resembled those of recorders. Unconsciously, as our focus moved through the edge of the knife blade and the wood again, the improvisation in the skies seeped into our minds.

With woodwind taken care of, we turned to other improvised instruments, a stick on a hollow log for a drum and a grass whistle. This is nothing more than a flat blade of grass, gripped between the heels and the tips of the thumbs pressed together. The space below the thumb knuckle acts as a natural mouthpiece, and with a little practice, a chirpy hoot emerges. Swapping between the different components of our woodland orchestra, notes rang in counterpoint to a strident robin redbreast. The rattling percussive call of magpies were as rhythmic as a metronome and we tried to keep up, one of us playing the elder whistles together, the other soloing on the kazoo-like grass blade. There were subtler sounds too: a blackbird's call rising and falling and a chiffchaff deeper in the trees squeaking like a rusty wheelbarrow. A cock pheasant in the fields clucked and hollered on the cooling air.

As sunlight gave way to a crepuscular glow, the woodland was flattened to a silhouette backdrop against the sky. Making music is medicine. It changes us so completely. We felt a pharmaceutical calmness descend as we walked to the wood's edge and watched for a while the dissipating light paint the trees and the wheat fields into blue, silver and ash-black. Suddenly the birdsong quieted too. Grey cloud drifted along the horizon like smoke and a lonely milk-white half-moon emerged. We struck up our whistles again, but the sky was empty. Above lay a prospect that stretched to the limits of our universe.

Autumn is the time when many birds begin their long migration south, gauging their bearings using the earth's magnetic fields to follow the sun. Swifts, martins, swallows and warblers, all seek out more agreeable spots, leaving only a few, like the robin, to defend their territory. Walking through a quiet, frozen landscape the absence of birds can seem a palpable void, which helps explain why encountering a robin sitting patiently on a bramble warms our hearts so: it is like meeting an old friend in an unfamiliar land. We reward its loyalty, decorating our Christmas cards with its image. How powerfully birds influence our lives and how little we realise.

The inspiration of their song has found expression in the instruments and musical development of all cultures and from the child's toy to the highest art. In India and China, whistles connected to a shallow container of water have been made to mimic varied birdcalls and songs for thousands of years. Beethoven was so charged by his love of nature that he once wrote to a friend, 'How happy I am to be able to walk among the shrubs, the trees, the woods, the grass and the rocks! For the woods, the trees and the rocks give man the resonance he needs.' The second movement of his 6th symphony ends with a series of cadenzas imitating the calls of the quail and the cuckoo.

Scientists have shown that at least some birds have to learn their songs from other birds of their species. A cardinal who has never heard a cardinal sing will not sound like one. This is particularly significant for bird species that turf other eggs out of nests to lay their own, such as the cuckoo. The resulting chicks are raised by foster parents of a different species, and have to learn the calls they should be making by congregating with other singing males and observing the reaction of females. In other words, each bird species has its own culture of musical improvisation. Passing information down the generations through song is probably not unique to birds: whales and dolphins may be doing it, and we do it too. The meanings of many nursery rhymes are scarcely relevant any more, indeed some are lost entirely, and yet they continue their slow evolution passed down between parents and children because there is still a deeply rooted reaction to their basic rhythm and gentle melody. It can be seen in the way we rock small children to sleep and instinctively speak to them in a singsong tone.

Perhaps because our ear is receptive to these comforting qualities, birdsong has been shown in some tests to improve recovery rates for patients and alleviate stress in general. Dr William Bird is the pioneer of the Green Gym where people improve their health by working to improve the environment. He believes fervently that: 'We have lost our connection with nature. By having birdsong, it's a way of connecting back, and our mental health improves when that connection has been made.' Certainly, our minds did not evolve to live removed from nature. Just like five fruit and veg a day can improve physical health, the small but repeated reconnection of exposure to birdsong can improve our mental wellbeing.

It is understandable then that its gradual disappearance can add a touch of melancholy to autumn evenings. There is a subconscious awareness that as the music winds down, the long dance of spring and summer must finally draw to a close. As winter bites, anyone who starts a commute before daybreak and returns after twilight can go through weeks of hardly seeing the sun. Then, around the time of the shortest day and even though winter is yet to fully release its grip, the migratory birds begin to return from epic journeys across open sea and scorching deserts to sing again. Each new morning heralds the latest performer returning triumphantly from their international tour and striking up on a branch. Listening to the burgeoning dawn chorus through a window tells us that spring is just around the corner. The days are lengthening. The season of new life is returning.

Making and playing a whistle in the woods allows us to keep something of this joy with us throughout the year. It is the same compulsion that saw unpaired male nightingales being kept in cages during medieval times, their singing filling the rooms with melody like primitive stereos. Bottling nature's notes in our borc-tree stems nourishes us through the cold months. It is the same joy of digging out a favourite album, the first chords of which transport us to another time; childhood memories, our first love or a summer holiday. For a moment at least, when you take the whistle from the shelf and blow it, the walls and furniture of the room fade away and you are back in the trees.

Music, both natural and manmade, holds a transformative power over us and has done so for millennia. Possibly the oldest instrument ever discovered is a bone flute made from the hollow wing of a vulture, and at over 40,000 years old it clearly shows that the process of forming note patterns and simple tones has been central to our existence for a very long time. There were almost certainly older instruments that have not survived, and before these, our hands would have clapped, and voices sung in unison. All art began in nature, and the first pigments and sounds might have had no more 'meaning' to them than evoking pleasure from the addition of bright colour or a clear tone. Or, like more figurative cave paintings, they might have reflected sounds in nature that brought strong emotions: birdsong for the coming of spring, the cries of animals in the hunt. Yet the complexity and powerful influence of music on the brain and body suggests something more. If music were only a reflection of nature it would merely mimic the sounds of leaves rustling in the breeze or waves crashing on the shore. Humans have instead shaped it over the centuries into the most affecting art form. We invest it with broader meanings: excitement, sadness, conflict and comfort. Just a few chords can resonate in our very bones and send a shiver down our spines, a smile to our faces or tears to our eyes.

In music and the delight of making instruments we see the manifestation of creativity itself. Ultimately the elder whistle maker knows that the note in the woods is like all expression, born out of the insatiable drive to leave a marker of our presence on earth, a statement of exist- ence, a way of saying 'I am here'. We watched our notes, our very breath made music, drift up into the great void; life blowing endlessly through the darkness.

Track an animal

All of us have seen the imprint of wild animals whether we have noticed them or not. The movement of nature around us is constantly recorded on the landscape and tracking is simply about learning to decipher and follow these patterns. A good enough reason alone for visiting the countryside, the skill to track animals is also knowledge that will enrich any time spent in the outdoors.

Snowy or muddy ground is best. Any time there is a fresh covering of snow, don't hesitate to get your boots on, especially if it is a shallow sheet of finer flakes. In deeper snow, animals tend to sink down into any drifts, their prints becoming indecipherable. Similarly, snow that is too wet or left for long can melt and refreeze, distorting any tracks or becoming too solid for lighter animals to leave any trace at all. But a few centimetres of fresh snowfall on top of a harder under-layer records perfectly the inky prints of everything that has crossed it. Even in the heart of a city, an overnight flurry may give you an easy-to-follow record of the wild animals in the area.

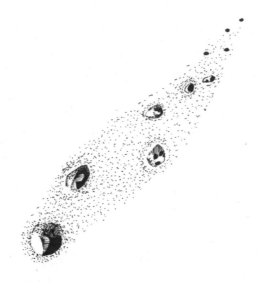

The best chance of success is to look in those places with the greatest population density of wildlife. Rural areas support a large range of herbivores and the nature of ecosystems means that wherever you find herbivores, you'll find carnivores too. Open ground provides little cover from predators and the most productive spots are invariably those that span two habitats: the field and forest, the forest and stream, the stream and field. If there is no snow, the bare, muddy areas of loamy soil favoured by farmers for growing crops also provide perfect conditions, so head for agricultural land fringed by woods, particularly after rain when the earth is softest. Fields that are occasionally flooded by a nearby river or stream are also likely to be moist and rich in the sort of silty earth that will take a print well.

Walk into the landscape and begin by tuning in. This is not as abstract a concept as you might think. Look around and ask yourself what features might influence your movements if you were an animal. Is there a road nearby, a house or a fence that will curtail your routes? Is there natural cover like hedging or trees you could use to travel safely? Shut your eyes and listen. Can you hear any animal calls? Which way is the wind blowing on your cheek? Look to see if there is a river or pond nearby where you could drink; tracks to a water source will invariably be along the easiest route. These are more than mere observations though: taking note of small details in this way for twenty minutes or so will not only give you the best places to look, it will instil the feeling of inner calm that is required to start tracking.

Walk slowly and quietly towards an area you have identified, trying to keep downwind where possible. Being lower in the sky, the winter sun casts long shadows. Arriving early in the morning or late in the afternoon, you can use this to your advantage, picking out tracks more easily by approaching towards the sun and sweeping the ground in front with your eyes. Look up every 10 metres or so. You will naturally see that certain areas stand out: oases of safety in a world of danger. Head towards any thicker tangles of grass, dry rushes, plants, reeds, roots, fallen wood or rocks. Near a food source, these spots provide safety and sustenance for wildlife.

As you move, keep an eye out for any markers of regular use or disturbance. Animals tend to take the simplest and most established travel routes unless hunting or escaping from a predator. Many therefore create 'runs', well-trodden paths used to access areas for feeding and breeding that will often have telltale clues such as flattened grass, broken stems, 'holes' that have been pushed through denser vegetation, clumps of hair trapped in barbed wire and droppings. They are often also rich with prints.

Other hot spots include anywhere that animals may be funnelled by a natural or manmade feature, especially around the gates of farmers' fields where the ground is usually churned up into a muddy soup by livestock. Look for bare patches of earth, clearings leading into woods and along footpaths. When rain has evaporated, tracks may also be found in and around dried puddles or in the mud, sand or silt by streams and riverbanks. In forests and woodland, ditches and paths free from fallen leaf litter are a good bet.

Sooner or later, you will find a print. Always start by identifying and recording it. In snow, making a drawing or taking a photograph is best, so carry a notebook, pen or mobile phone with a camera just in case. Drawing forces you to look and study each print more carefully, which may help with the nuances of identification. When photographing, include something to add scale, a coin perhaps or a matchbox.

In mud or sand, it is always worth trying to take a cast of a good print. This can capture details of the shape unseen from the surface – claws and hair for instance – and allows you to study it more closely at home. All you need is some thin card, an old jam jar three-quarters filled with cold water, some sticky tape and a small bag of Plaster of Paris. This can be bought at most hardware stores, builder's merchants or art shops and is best decanted into a dry, screw-top container that can be carried around with you. An old 500-millilitre plastic water bottle will do.

Cut the card into a strip that will comfortably encircle the print, 10 or 12 centimetres in width. Stick the two ends together to form a loop that should fit over the track with a little clearance on all sides. If needs be, stick two bits of card together to get the right size. Push the circle into the ground, forming a barrier to prevent the plaster leaking out.

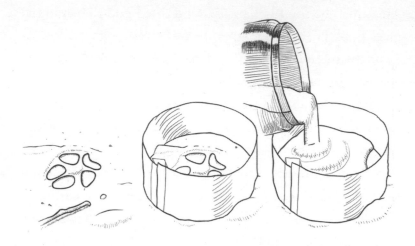

Gradually add the Plaster of Paris to the cold water in the jam jar. Keep stirring it with a thin stick and add more water until the consistency starts to resemble pancake batter. Get ready and hover over the print, pouring the plaster into the centre carefully but quickly. Let the plaster come up the card a few centimetres and then stop. It will take around 20 minutes to set and 45 minutes before it is strong enough to be removed.

In the meantime, follow the prints as far as you can to see what stories unfold. Record what happens and where they go. What animal is it? Are the prints joined or intersected by other tracks? Do they lead to signs of a kill or of an escape into the undergrowth? Walk with the tracks, but be careful not to obscure them. If you lose the trail, try moving out from the last print in concentric circles until you pick it up again. With deer or foxes, you might find the trail goes on for miles, but with each step you become more consumed by the pleasure of tracing the animal's movement, establishing empathy with and drawing you closer to the wild itself. Perhaps the search means you have to leave the footpath or route you had intended to follow that day, but this isn't a bad thing. Tracking animals naturally leads us into a world that strips away the sanitised layers of modern life. It enriches and educates with every encounter.

We sat patiently at the top of a small slope littered with rabbit holes by the edge of a field. Our eyes were fixed on the track 20 metres or so below. The trees groaned and creaked in the gusting January breeze like ships' timbers in a storm as the first trace of dusk smudged the sky. To be in a wood as dark approaches is a strange sensation. Instinct says it is unnatural and unsafe, and it was as though the waving trees were ushering us from a place that grew darker and colder by the minute, back to the comforting fire of the Welsh cottage we were staying in. Although we were hunkered down and hidden among the leaves, everything seemed to be watching us. Even a blink felt like a clumsy betrayal of our presence. The life we had disturbed getting into position started to return after half an hour. Our still-ness was accepted. First came the birds, wood pigeons and rooks fluttering in to roost among the fizzing branches of the beeches. Blue tits hopped among the shrubbier, younger silver birch and, breaking out of their chattering throng, treecreepers spiralled up the bark of the more established trees in search of a meal. Brown and white balls of feathers, they shimmered up trunks so quickly it looked like the trees themselves were waking up and stretching.

Only a few hours before, under a pale, watery winter sun, we had found the footprint lying in a muddy furrow that ran parallel to the farmer's track we were now watching. At first we took it for a dog, but on inspection it was too long and slender, about 5 centimetres from heel to claw and 4 centimetres wide. The telltale difference was a clear space between the front two pads and the outer pair; a matchstick placed between touched neither. In a dog, this would have bisected them. There was also a larger gap between the front pads and the heel pad. With dogs, they are bunched up together. The wetness of the soft mud was such that even the imprint of the hair a fox carries between its toes at this time of year had been pressed gently into the ground.

A bit further and we found another print and another, all following the same strangely oblique pattern a fox adopts when trotting, positioning its body diagonally to the line it is following. The smell was intense, a musky sourness that is hard to forget, and with each step we drew closer to the animal that had left it. Retracing its movements through the vegetation meant lowering ourselves to the ground and we saw, as Ted Hughes did, that 'delicately as the dark snow, a fox's nose touches twig, leaf'. It wasn't hard to see the reason why. The evidence of rabbits was everywhere; the tree-strewn banks pockmarked with holes and excavated earth of an ochre colour, flashes of brightness among the leafy brown topsoil. Warrens act as natural auditoriums, each hole a trumpet that draws in and magnifies the sounds from outside. The effect is most resonant at the entrances and naturally rabbits emerge and pause to listen there, leaving a concentration of droppings and prints for the switched-on tracker to find. We resolved to return and lie in wait, hopeful of watching a drama unfold.

Darkness had almost completely fallen when we heard the crash of undergrowth. Rabbits disturbed while making their way to the fields for supper were dashing into bushes of holly. The sudden noise elicited a sharp intake of breath and we peered around the hollow of the tree beside us. On the path below was a fox, frozen in the half-light. It looked up at us and sniffed the air, staring. We are all familiar with urban foxes out at night, jumping over a wall to get at dustbins or ravaging a black bin bag for some leftover chicken, but in this environment it seemed as different a species as a wolf is to a dog. Cloaked in the trees, this was a thick-maned wild animal and we were trespassers in its kingdom. For a few moments we locked eyes before, with a yawn and a sniff, it was off, back into the blackness.

From childhood, we are encouraged to appreciate nature in the grand sense, the majesty of mountain views, sea vistas and sweeping landscapes, but that evening we found that there is just as much reward from focusing on the small-scale. Tracking is a process of decoding symbols. Initially meaningless, we learn to identify prints singly at first, just like individual letters. With only a

little practice, they work together to become full words that describe an action. As you grow more familiar with them, series of tracks can appear like sentences telling you a detailed story, enabling you to read the terrain in a different, more fulfilling and fascinating way. By simply taking the time to look more closely at the forest floor, we had found a fox print and traced its trail. From this single letter, we had been given a mysterious narrative to follow. We were even able to return and see the fox, which had instilled in us both an unexpected empathy with a wild animal we had previously regarded in a very different light. Neither of us had expected the rush of adrenaline in our chests at the sight of a fox, but this was no mangy-coated, dull-eyed invader of the suburban sprawl. It seemed to be born out of the trees and copper earth, a manifestation of the dark wood itself, soft-padding through the night. Our walk back to the warm cottage was in silence. We wondered where the fox's footsteps were being left now, as the mournful 'twit-twoo' calls of tawny owls rang out across the moonlit fields, the frost a crystal sheen over the grass.

Once experienced, the urge to hunt for prints cannot be quickly switched off. The next morning we struck out early to scour the fields and woods adjacent to a river nearby, eager to use the rainfall we'd heard during the night to our advantage in trying to track that most elusive of creatures, the badger. Being nocturnal and therefore mostly unseen, there is something ghostly about the footprints of a badger. They are a trace of the night itself, the five toes and claws resembling a miniature bear stalking across the land. The toe pads are close together in a row and along with the heel pad form a print that measures about 5 centimetres long and 4 centimetres wide. Badgers tend to lollop along, placing their hind prints on top of their fore prints, so it is common to see the two tracks superimposed. If followed to their sett, they are best observed half an hour before dawn or dusk, when lying downwind and a good distance away. A rustle in the undergrowth gives way to an indistinct shape in the dim light, hard to place at first but quickly resolving into that famous striped, monochrome visage.

Entering a narrower stretch of the river valley, thick with trees, our eyes darted down dark passageways to any areas of moist ground with good cover. A few steps into a copse, the silt had formed a perfect inch-thick layer of muck to receive prints, the fresh stamp of a boot and dog track indicating the conditions were absolutely perfect. Leaving the path, we delved deeper into remarkable tree formations created by the flooding and subsequent collapse of the banks. Some trunks arched high across our path, while others jutted horizontally. Unearthly avenues through the ancient Welsh land brought to mind visions of the vast array of beasts that once stalked our island before being hunted into oblivion by man. Now, in the place of bears, lynx and wolves, more familiar signs appeared; fox, dog and rabbit prints ran over each other in hectic patterns. We followed them into the undergrowth.

The higher ground to our right was perfect terrain for a badger sett: any rainwater would drain away from the sloping bank, it had plenty of open wood and easy access to fields behind for worms and grubs. We moved silently into the birch, looking for prints and the unmistakable entrance architecture of a badger sett: a hole lying like the letter 'D' on its side. A fence ran along the field boundary and we checked each knot of barbed wire for clumps of hair where they might have ducked under to do some snuffling. White in colour with a black band towards the tip, badger hair is easy to distinguish. It is oval in cross-section so when rolled between thumb and forefinger it feels angular, like rolling a tiny pencil rather than a perfectly round tube.

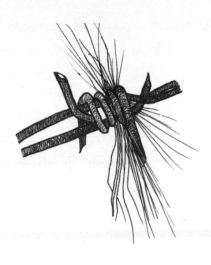

Looping our way back to the silent moving mass of the river, we were distracted by a sheer but small drop to the water. It ended in a tiny beach, just over a metre long, formed from collapsed mud and deposited silt. Perhaps if we'd just been strolling through the landscape, neither of us would have registered it, but having been tuned in to our surroundings all morning, we got the sense that we should look over. There, as plain as a picture, were two prints. The webbed feet were so clear you could immediately tell the exact form of the front and rear track, and even the angle at which the animal must have paused before slipping into the river. There was no need to check characteristics such as size or shape; it was unmistakably an otter.

These rare prints were a valuable lesson that tracking is both active and passive. We had ventured out with a definite quarry and been unsuccessful, but by being in the right frame of mind and taking the time to look, something even more special had presented itself. Neither of us spoke for a minute as we processed the value of our discovery, then we hurriedly began preparing to cast the prints. Suddenly something splashed into the water along the bank. Hidden from view among the cover of some fallen trees, it sounded large and we turned, hoping to catch a glimpse of the most shy of British mammals, but whatever it was, it was too skilled and stealthy a swimmer. Still, we now had an inkling as to how recently our prints may have been left, and crouching down to inspect them more carefully found another detail that confirmed it. Tiny water droplets had made a fan of minuscule craters in the sand. Positioned ahead of the front paw, they gave the distinct impression they had been shaken by a sharp turn of the otter's head. It was here only seconds before us.

The joy of taking casts when tracking any animal is that this kind of encounter stays with you physically as well as emotionally. Sitting on a windowsill in a living room or on a desk in an office, the webbed paw of an otter in relief gives a very real sense of connection to an animal in a way a photograph never can. It is a tactile reminder of its claws, flesh and character, still coated in the grains of sandy silt the print was found in. Holding it feels like shaking hands with the creature.

Establishing such a physical yet non-intrusive connection is important. Society has engendered a 'look don't touch' mentality with wild animals and, while in many cases this is for good reason, it creates a paradox. Our minds have evolved to track; the innate desire to follow and understand how wildlife moves, lives and interacts is present in every child who lifts a rock to watch the bugs, beetles and other beasties scuttle away. Indeed for early humans, it was a skill essential to life. Our ancestors would follow the prints of lions and their prey for many miles to find fresh kills, before driving off the predators in groups and scavenging the meat. Early human hunters depended on herds of wild game, even moving with them as they migrated to avoid starvation, with some theories suggesting we were first drawn out of Africa and began to populate the wider world as a result. Men hunted with poisoned arrows that took time to work into the animal's bloodstream, meaning the ability to read the wounded beasts' movements for great distances in terrain criss-crossed by similar prints was paramount. As we found when tracking the fox, adopting the character of the animal and simulating its movement is the best way to stay on its trail. It is a technique practised still by tribesmen in Africa today.

The way in which our ancestors once lived or died by the strength of their interaction with and knowledge of wildlife can be seen in the incredible detail of 30,000-year-old cave paintings. The animals portrayed sometimes have their hooves or paws turned at odd angles to face the viewer, revealing their composition as more than just decorative. They are teaching aids for tracking. If we spend a little time memorising small differences, we may distinguish between the prints of similar animals that surround us. Take deer, for example. All have a cloven footprint, but each species also has its own qualities too. Fallow deer can be identified by their long, pointed, narrow prints. Bucks will leave a track around 8 centimetres long and 5 centimetres wide, with the doe's measuring 5 to 6 centimetres long and 3 to 4 centimetres wide, both showing little sign of splaying. A roe deer print, on the other hand, can be recognised by the tendency of the pointed cleaves to splay outwards, especially when galloping or clearing an obstacle such as a hedge or fence. Other features include its small size in both buck and doe, around 4.5 centimetres long and 3 centimetres wide, and the fact that the prominent rear 'dew' claws are often visible. Red deer, the largest wild animal in Britain, have an unmistakably broad print, the outer edges of the cleaves turning evenly towards the tip, seeming rounded and almost like the heel print of a boot. The forefoot measures 8 or 9 centimetres in length and 6 or 7 centimetres wide and will often splay out when galloping or jumping.

Keeping a record of prints like these where we find them, whether by drawing, photographing or casting, helps to re-establish something of the reverential relationship we find in ancient cave paintings, one that still finds expression today in the way we name our cars: the Puma, the Jaguar, the Mustang. Interestingly, however, our brains do not respond to modern hazards like a dangerous road crossing in the same way as we still respond to the threats we evolved alongside. A coiled rope seen out of the corner of one eye can still cause a momentary freeze and a rush of adrenaline as our lower brain mistakes it for a snake, yet the smooth motion of a far more dangerous road vehicle does not have the same effect.

We evolved to have a hands-on and active engagement with the wild animal, yet for many of us, our only connection now is through the filter of a screen. The watcher has replaced the hunter. Wildlife documentaries bring us closer to animals we would never otherwise learn about. They astound us with the unknown and give us sights that would take a lifetime of dedication to achieve for ourselves, but alone they are not enough. Nature at its rawest is not something that can just be enjoyed from the comfort of an armchair. It must be experienced firsthand.

Viewing even the most fascinating television documentary is a cerebral process removed from being out in the fields and forests. Tracking forces us to engage with the physicality of the outdoors; it is a 360° sensory experience. It goes beyond just processing the images in front of us, it is the rush of adrenaline on finding a track, the release of endorphins lying in wait, the anticipation and excitement of seeing a wild animal in its natural terrain. Whereas on television, volume levels are compressed and constant, there is a rich depth and subtlety to the sounds of nature. Even the light and detail from the best HD screen is comparatively limited and unchanging. It cannot possibly match the dynamic range of natural luminescence and the little details our eyes notice when outside. Think of the very dark shadows of a wood and the starlit sky, the effect of dusk falling or the slightest movement. Unlike a screen, these engender a physical transformation. Our eyes change from using cones to rods, and a natural night vision kicks in that is a far more effective motion sensor. The peripheral vision takes over and seasoned trackers know to never look at something directly in the dark, as it will disappear when you move any image on to the cone-rich fovea region of the eye.

Tracking elicits a physiological as well as psychological change, one that brings us closer to every landscape. We connect on another level, down among the leaves. Perhaps at the heart of this ancient art is this sense of 'becoming' with the landscape and its inhabitants. In

Wales, we learnt that this is something that can be gained through as little as sitting in silence as dusk falls. Lao Tzu, philosopher and founder of Taoism, said: 'No thought, no action, no movement, total stillness: only thus can one manifest the true nature and law of things from within and unconsciously, and at last become one with heaven and earth.'

We spend so much of our lives trying to cut out the sensory overload and it can be a remarkable sensation letting it fill every corner of our minds, letting the internal monologue slow and then cease and shifting to living in the present moment. This state of contemplation, sitting in a natural environment as the day moves, deciphering the symbols around us, watching the gradual changes of the sky, hearing the sounds of plants and animals alike, gives us new eyes.

We often forget that we too are animals, trying to build a home and a place in the world, leaving our marks here and there with varying levels of transience. When we understand the most basic forces in life, it cannot help but lead us towards thinking of our own footprints. What will we leave behind for others to follow?

Build a den

Turning fallen wood and loose leaves into a home from home, a place that will keep you warm and dry overnight, needn't require chainsaw or axe. In fact, a basic debris den can be made quickly in almost any woodland with nothing but your bare hands.

The first thing to do is to choose a good spot. Somewhere with lots of leaf litter and dead wood makes the job easiest. The important thing is to find a clear area that is at least twice as big as the proposed shelter, which will be roughly one and a half times your body length when lying down. Lie on the ground and try the space out for size and comfort, avoiding any roots or patches of uneven earth. Look up and take notice of what is above you. Falling branches can be a serious hazard, especially in windy conditions. Beech trees have been known to suddenly drop a sizeable branch in dry weather to save water, and while a stately oak tree is less likely to shed its appendages, you should stay on the safe side. Avoid setting up camp too close to the trunk of any large tree.

Next, start collecting your key pieces: two sticks about the same size, a metre in length and around 7 to 10 centimetres in diameter that both fork into a 'Y'-shaped end. These will create your entrance and bear most of the weight so choose strong, sturdy branches that fit together well. Prop them against one another, using the divisions at the end to interlink them before looking for the third piece of the frame: a long spine to sit on top that will create a triangular pyramid. This will dictate the size of the internal area so it needs to be longer than you. Lay it across both the interlocked 'Y' shapes and test the whole thing for stability. If it feels secure, check you can get your whole body inside, including a 30-centimetre gap from your head to the entrance as changing it later will undo much of the work. Is there enough room for your feet to stick straight up towards the tapered end? Can you get yourself in through the triangular entrance easily? Remember, a den perfectly tailored to its occupant is best, so if you're making a child-sized shelter, start with a smaller initial frame.

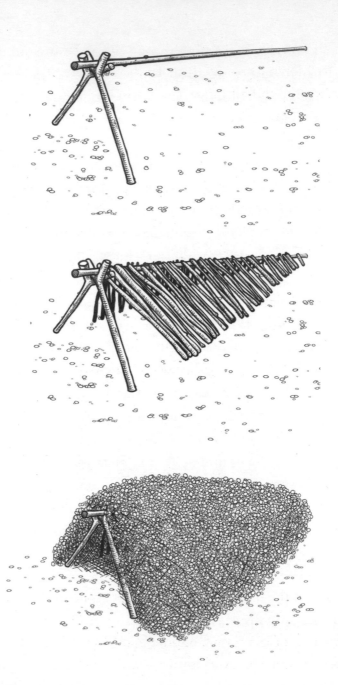

To cover it, first collect lots of sticks ranging from a metre down to about 10 centimetres in length. Place the longest at the entrance and work your way along the spine, covering each side. Site them a few centimetres apart and point the tops slightly forward towards the entrance. Make sure the sticks are close enough together so a leaf litter covering won't fall through and that they project no more than a few centimetres over the spine. Those that do will provide a pathway for rain to trickle in. Once these 'ribs' are in place, lay smaller twigs on top. Don't be too fussy, but loosely hook and weave any little kinks and spindly side branches in between to create a rough lattice.

When the den has an equal covering all around, start burying it in great bundles of leaf litter. Pile armfuls on the sides of the frame, building up from the bottom and over the spine in layers until the whole thing is covered by debris to at least a depth of 40 centimetres. It may take a little time, but this thick layer will provide insulation and waterproofing as effectively as anything manmade. Finally, lay some light, dead branches over the top to hold the covering in place. If trying to save time or short on leaves, a tarpaulin will cover just as well, but you lose the pleasure of creating a den that blends back into the woodland. Why cut yourself off from nature with a layer of plastic? Better to put the tarpaulin down on the inside. Body heat is lost through contact with the cold ground, so when sleeping in a den, it is a good idea to use a foam mat as well as a sleeping bag.

As soon as we entered the Cornish wood, we felt less exposed to the April air. There is almost a sense of being inside when among the trees or, at least, some other half-way state between indoors and outdoors. From the fields beyond, it was an impenetrable green mass, but stepping through the bordering thickets of holly and hawthorn suddenly there was concealed space. Rooms stretched beyond rooms, each a separate shape and design. It was like a natural Tardis, or pushing through the fur coats of the wardrobe into C. S. Lewis's Narnia. The leaves muffled much of the sound of the lively spring wind, and there was a sense of still closeness very different from being in the open fields beyond. We felt almost as though we'd walked in on the beech, sycamore and oak in intense conversation, our footsteps hushing them into whispers. Falling silent for a moment, the sense of reverence was akin to that which preacher Henry Ward Beecher noted, 'Of all men's works of art, a cathedral is the greatest. A vast and majestic tree is greater than that.' Monuments surrounded us, but with none of the impersonal coldness of some places of worship. The high ceiling of the canopy was church-like, vaulted and flooded with diffused light; natural stained glass in the bright sunshine. Beneath, the ground was softly carpeted with leaves. A nearby stump provided a stool, a fallen trunk a bench. This was a spot as old as England and, like stumbling upon a mystical hollow down a forgotten track, we were entranced.

Abandoning our hike for the day, we set about putting the dead wood all around to good use. The ground was dry and we lay on the crisp brown leaves of last autumn's fall to measure out the space for two dens. We agreed they should face each other with a small area of shared soil between which could hold a fire if the day grew cold. Dimensions and layout decided it was time to find the logs to interlock that would create our elongated tripod frames. One of the great things about building such rudimentary shelters is the speed of their construction. Within fifteen minutes, both of our frames were in place and we had set to collecting sticks to rest along their sides. It was easy to gather as many dry branches of various sizes and thickness as we could and dump them in one shared heap. Trying each stick for size we could see which ones fit best, returning those that didn't or placing them somewhere else along the spine. The competition to finish first was unspoken but continued as we progressed to heaping mounds of leaf litter and damp brown earthy mould over the top, only the occasional load lost in childish attacks on one another. Perhaps because of the play or the distraction of exploring our otherworldly dell, the covering took the best part of an hour and a half. Eventually, though, we could plunge our arms up to the elbow in the thick layers of leaves and the dens were weatherproof. And just in time. The sky had darkened and a spattering of rain rattled the crowns of the trees. We hurriedly took shelter inside our new homes, lying on our bellies and looking out, as the bit of common ground between poured with run-off from the oaks.

To crawl inside a debris den is to be inside the very earth. The rudimentary rafters disappear down towards your feet in a simple, pleasing uniformity, lying interspersed with tactile pockets of musty, brown humus. Surprising, perhaps, is the warmth and the quiet. Even when the rain had passed, we lay in the dens as the forest came to life again; our eyes shut, cocooned in the atmospheres we had enclosed.

Unlike putting up a tent, which very definitely sits on top of the ground, and clearly defines internal and external, a leaf litter shelter is more like climbing under a giant eiderdown, lifting the ground up. Because you are shaping the woodland itself, it takes on that same character of being both indoors and outdoors. You are sheltered, covered in leaf litter in more than one sense, and yet if anything you are closer to the earth than when you started, sinking into the ground itself. Once experienced, it becomes like a secret room, one that exists in every wood if you have the inclination to conjure it.

As these seemingly magical skills develop, the temptation is to try new tricks, experimenting with other types of construction. No architect would be content with building in the same style for ever. In an area of forest close to Arundel, given over by its landlord to bushcraft activities and run by a friendly woodsman, we had the chance. West Sussex is a complex layering of the traditional and progressive, ancient and modern, and our journey had taken us past picturesque houses overlooked by a mighty castle, but as we abandoned our vehicles and set out across fields towards the stand of trees, all began to fade away. The wind blew back towards the nearest road and the drone of traffic disappeared. Ducking beneath branches revealed a complete absence of noise. To be in any quiet wood is a sensory shift. Ears soon adjust to the calls of birds and the snap and shuffle of feet on leaves.

All around us, endless coppiced hazel sprouted from cut-back stumps in slender sprays. The young branches of this mainstay of British forests are incredibly flexible, and the roundish, gently serrated leaves waved freely in the breeze. With such an abundance of material, it was time to try a slightly more ambitious construct than our debris dens: a 'bender' or 'wikiup' tall enough to stand in.

Wandering among hazel, accompanied by occasional birch, yew and ash, we stepped carefully through dense carpets of bluebells in sunny clearings. The slants of light picking out the purplish blooms and hovering yellow motes against the green of the leaves gave the woods a fantastical quality. We could quite believe we had entered the world of *A Midsummer Night's Dream* 'where the bolt of Cupid fell/ . . . upon a little western flower,/Before milk-white, now purple with love's wound,/And maidens call it love-in-idleness'. Here and there along the path a pale yellow primrose stood in contrast to the blue, and hoverflies pottered between them, their striped attempts to mimic wasps betrayed by their angular flight paths and sudden suspension in the air.

We were being just as industrious with our folding saws. Because the poles we needed had to be both long and flexible, we were obliged to look carefully at the candidates. Older growths were plenty long enough, but could be three or more centimetres thick at the base and far too sturdy for us to bend into shape. Younger sprouts might be too short, or even too thin. As with picking out pieces for any shelter, it paid to spend more time considering where to cut than cutting.

The close observation led us through archways between drooping boughs. We had entered a mode of thought where the treescape was no longer a closed book. It was living history, recounting tales of its planting and management. The pattern of recent years was quite clear. Trees that are coppiced or cut down to ground level continually regrow from the remaining trunk base or 'stool'. The new young trunks are every bit as active and energetic as the first seedling. Regular coppicing means a tree will never die of old age; an occasional trim is a small gift to pay for eternal life. Some original trunks are centuries old and many metres across, yet still produce fresh shoots as perfect as the first. The more distant past of this wood, dating back to the 1600s at least, was also beneath our fingers and boots. It was buried deep in the ringed heart of the proudest oaks and the thick covering of bluebells.

We cut thirty hazel saplings, trimmed them of smaller branches and buds, made a circle of twelve holes in the ground and placed the tallest from our haul inside them. Between the uprights, we weaved two horizontal rows, binding tightly at the touch points with twine, like a very loose wattle. Bending the supple tops inwards, we tied pairs of uprights together to make a series of arches. Finally, the three verticals at either end were bent inwards and tied across the central arches in various places to make a complete dome. If the knotting is secure, and the branches are fresh green wood, a structure of this type can last for many years. It takes rather more effort than a debris shelter, and requires sufficient young saplings and a saw, but is better as a semi-permanent residence. The native Americans, from whom the name 'wikiup' comes, would cover such frames with anything from grasses and rushes to purpose-cut cloth or hide. There being not nearly enough bison roaming the fields of West Sussex, we plumped for a huge camouflage-green tarpaulin.

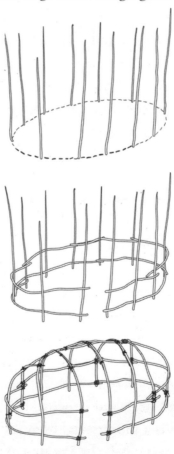

Spend time studying trees and it is not very long before a large trunk, far beyond the size we wanted to fell, presents a likely looking branch – not for den making but as a handhold. Climbing trees is an essential art and a tempting distraction. One theory about the sudden sense of falling we sometimes feel before jolting awake in bed is that it stems from a need to prevent ourselves slipping out of the branches while taking a nap, a legacy from when we still took to the trees for safety at night. The tactile quality of finding purchase makes the sense of touch intrinsic. We commune with the wood by proxy. As children, climbing a tree is enough for us to feel a sense of being transported away from grown-ups below. We climb to the crow's nest to see a world that stretches out before us, like the future.

Even when we are adults, trees and woods can help us to just *be*. Once a shelter is built, the normal patterns of life, eating, sleeping and socialising can be re-established in a different context. We merge our existence with the wood by performing the small rituals that make up the everyday. We go to bed when darkness falls and rise with the light. We tap into the deeper rhythms of the earth. Sleeping in the outdoors, without the impermeable double membrane of a tent, we slip into a state of immersion. The woods have a life independent of us, a slow, powerful existence that Tolkien captured in his talking trees, the Ents: 'Treebeard marched on, . . . after a time, his voice died to a murmur and fell silent again . . . his old brow was wrinkled and knotted. At last he looked up, and Pippin could see a sad look in his eyes, sad but not unhappy. There was a light in them, as if the green flame had sunk deeper into the dark wells of his thoughts.' We can walk with the trees for a time, but something about their presence reminds us that they pre-date our existence and will outlast us too. Staying overnight among their roots builds an emotional bond. Spending longer in the woods or returning to the same spot, we can watch the trees change from season to season, from walking among the first buds of spring, to waking in woodland silenced by snow.

Profound roots and tall branches connect the under-world beneath the ground with the heavens. Shamans spoke of their power to bridge past and future. Physically, you can find holes at the base of some oak trunks that seem to wind down into impenetrable depths, or you can climb up to where the canopy becomes a sea rolling before you in the wind. Metaphorically, the connections between the underworld and paradise expressed by trees crop up in the biblical story of the two trees in paradise. The Tree of Life is a motif in many religions and mythol-ogies. Egyptian depictions of Isis, goddess of motherhood, sometimes showed her as a sycamore tree; Yggdrasil, the world tree, was a huge ash in Scandinavian myth, with roots linking the lands of mortals and of the gods; Buddha is said to have sat beneath the Bodhi Tree, a fig, when he gained enlightenment, and Buddhists still visit its descendants to commune with them. The ability of trees to yield cuttings from which will grow new adults may also be tied up in the parthenogenesis of many ancient gods, springing from their parents without birth.

The urge to make dens is present in us from childhood. Whether out in the trees or under a few blankets stretched between chairs in a living room, we feel the need to construct our own private space to get away from everything. This can be seen in the way every child shrieks with joy to see a humble treehouse, but may gaze uninterested at the greatest architectural wonders on our planet. Like dens, treehouses offer a combination of being somewhere very different from the home, but being close enough to rejoin the safety of family when we so desire. It is life on the perimeter, somewhere we can establish our own rules of habitation: the unknown place to go with friends, hidden to the untrained eye, the secret password, the place to stash keepsakes. As night falls the excitement builds, the walls of the den become a sanctuary on the frontier.

As adults in Britain, we know we're never too far from civilisation, but when we are sleeping outdoors as night falls, every second becomes memorable. Our minds are saturated with subtle changes, the cold descending, the light shifting, daytime creatures turning in and the night watch emerging. The dark tranquillity found in any wooded area is profound; you turn off your torch and are reduced to the level of our ancestors, imagining what lies beyond the veil of night.

But when snug in your den and sleeping bag, the unfamiliar sounds of the forest, the creak of trees, the rustle of leaves, gradually become a comforting background, lulling you to sleep. By the time you wake up, everything is a reconnecting experience. Even a morning lie-in, normally a way to shut out the reality of having to take on the world or the rest of the week, is instead a gradually building delight. In our wikiup, sunlight filtered through the leaves and the shelter's covering, twice softened by this passage, and gently dappled the interior. Birdsong layered in the air. A greater spotted woodpecker was providing percussion overhead. A blackbird was belting out a soaring solo. A string section was provided by blue tits and great tits, and the firm brassy notes of a collared dove.

Whether it is in a cosy hollow, built up against a sturdy trunk or raised into the branches, a woodland den is a fantastic way to get a more intimate experience of this realm. We are outside the day-to-day, in a different world, and can cast a measured, objective eye back towards the land beyond the trees. Problems we thought towered above us are diminished in comparison to the solid form of oak and ash. We become treelike in our outlook, calmer and more stately. Being in the woods, the woods naturally are in you. Roger Deakin described it wonderfully. 'I am well on the way to becoming a tree myself. I put down roots. I sigh when the wind blows. My sap rises in spring. I turn towards the sun. My skin even begins to look more like bark every day.'

Personification of trees can be seen in the dryads and hamadryads of myth. Some nymphs were intrinsically linked to particular species, like the Meliads: ash trees sprung from the sky god's blood. The reverse arboreal transformation is also common: Daphne turned into a laurel as she fled from Apollo; Baucis and Philemon transformed into oak and linden, twining their branches eternally as a symbol of their love. These stories would have imbued the plants people encountered with a range of special significances and interest, even after belief in the myths themselves had faded.

Once you can identify a dozen types of tree, a forest or area of parkland ceases to be a dense, incomprehensible curtain of leaves. Each individual presents itself as a specimen of a particular type and may be as different from its neighbour as any two people are from one another. Further encounters bring an appreciation of how a particular tree stands out from others of its kind. They tell tales of careful stewardship or unkempt industry. They may be gangly victors of an unforgiving race to the sun in a dense coppice, or comfortably proportioned parkland gentry, or broad-chested sentinels guarding the mouth of a river.

Suddenly, entering a wood becomes akin to returning home. Familiar things surround you again, and other demands on your attention fall away. Trees are old friends that do not ask for our time; we are completely free to give it as we wish. They are the opposite of the animals we keep as pets – smaller, more frenetic and shorter-lived than us. Just as a domesticated companion can help support our love of living in the now, of activity, of relating to another, so spending time with the trees speaks to us of weathering the storm, of adapting without judgement to the seasons and environment around us, of accepting the arc of time beyond.

Even in your back garden, where there may be no centuries-old oaks or quick-growing hazel, find enough sticks and you can make a den. This allows you to unlock something you already had, but perhaps never realised: the stillness of your garden at night, the furtive movements of nocturnal animals, the pale dawn met by birdsong as you lie wrapped in what John Stewart Collis called 'the soft arms of the earth'. Nowadays we are all exposed to an impetus to get our own place. We work a whole lifetime to earn this place. It is the single biggest investment many of us make, putting in untold hours of effort in order to feel that sense of excitement at taking ownership only a handful of times. It is a mind-expanding experience to return to the roots of this desire, to connect oneself to it directly rather than through an intermediary. Going outside with the firm intention of sleeping the night in a den can engender the same sense of pride, satisfaction and pleasure as buying our dream house.

We should not get caught up arbitrarily valuing the natural over the unnatural though. After all, what is 'natural'? Almost every inch of Britain has been worked over at some point, even if only to preserve its existing characteristics. A coppiced wood, unnaturally cut back, displays a greater diversity of plants, animals, birds and insects than an area left to grow at will. Unless you believe humans to be fundamentally unnatural, then even such wonders as the pyramids, brain surgery, or getting people to the moon and back are ultimately products of nature. But civilisation is a paradox; created by us, it takes us out of the terrains we evolved to live in. Dwelling in houses is a relatively recent change for humans. Specialising as everything from farmers, factory workers or brokers of information may have yielded great benefits, but we all still have the instinct to fulfil our desires physically with what is to hand. We are all trying to make a better den.

Light a fire

There are only four things required to light a fire: heat, fuel, oxygen and permission from the landowner, but the last must always come first. Make sure you have the OK from whoever's garden or wood you are using and that you are fully complying with the law in any open space.

Find a bit of ground that is flat and sheltered, but with enough gentle breeze to provide the oxygen. The heart of a forest will provide a ready source of fuel, and in summer the wood is more likely to be dry. Keep far enough away from any trees to prevent even the slightest damage to trunks, branches or root systems. A minimum of 5 metres should do it, but base your decision on how large the trees are, and remember their root systems will be about as wide as their branches.

Start by taking a mental snapshot of the ground.

When you leave this spot, it must look identical. The true skill in making fire is not the lighting, but the leaving; it should be impossible for someone passing by to tell that you have been there. Scrape a metre-and-a-half circle down through the leaf litter to the bare earth. If you are in a garden or on grass, use a spade or knife to cut away the turf in a square about the same size, roll it up carefully and store it a safe distance away. The ground can be well watered afterwards and the turf replaced with no damage. In fact, nitrogen from the ash can stimulate growth. Don't make the classic mistake of lining the circle with stones; these will do nothing to contain the fire, and they may even explode when moisture is heated in cracks within the rock.

Next collect your materials: tinder, kindling, and fuel of various sizes. Roam over as wide a distance as you can to avoid clearing any one bit of the woodland completely. The tinder needs to be bone-dry material with plenty of surface area that will catch a spark easily. Birch bark is perhaps the most famous natural tinder, being plentiful and flaring up bright and hot, kick starting the combustion of the surrounding fuel. The silver birch tree is also very easy to recognise and common in gardens and woods. Thanks to its relatively fast growth and attractive weeping foliage shape, it is also a favourite on residential streets. Look for its small, green, triangular leaves with serrated edges and its straight trunk, a distinctive silvery-white in colour with occasional black splits. Peel off the fraying exterior bark from the living trees; it should come away in light, thin, papery strips, and you will need a good couple of pocketfuls. Dead birch is equally useful, although the bark will come away in thicker sections.

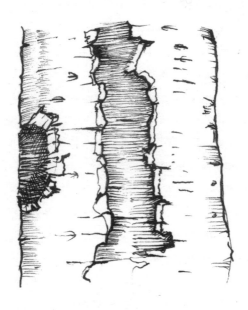

Next comes the kindling. Begin with twigs of match-stick-thickness, ideally around 30 centimetres in length, snapped from standing dead wood. Most of the wood you find on the ground is wet or rotten, but to test it, touch it against your cheek. We are more sensitive to moisture on our faces than through our fingers and, if it feels like a gentle kiss, leave it. Fallen branches on the undersides of trees are excellent places to look, as they are usually drier, even if it has rained recently. Don't snap longer sticks into shorter bundles, as their length provides manoeuvrability when the fire is lit, giving greater control. When you have collected two bunches, each as big as you can hold in one hand, progress on to wood that is pencil-thickness and so on, doubling the width each time until you reach slim log-sized wood that is just shy of the span of your wrist. Now comes the important part. However much you have, force yourself to go out and double the amount. In our eagerness to get a fire going, we all too often underestimate the amount of fuel required.

Make a fire platform in the centre of the circle. This will insulate the tinder from the ground and form a good base of charcoal and hot ash as it burns. Take note of the way the wind is blowing by wetting your finger and holding it up or throwing some leaf litter into the air. Use sticks between 30 and 40 centimetres in length and lay them tightly together on the ground perpendicular to the wind until you have a roughly square and level platform.

The papery, living birch bark can simply be torn into thin strips until it resembles a bushy bird's nest. Place this soft, fluffy mass at the heart of the platform. Don't compress it, as the air needs plenty of room to circulate.

If you are using bark from a dead tree, scrape the blade of a pocketknife towards you across the exterior side of a large piece to create shavings and dust. Keep going until there is a mound a few centimetres high and put the whole thing on to the fire platform. Tear the remaining bark up, hold it between two hands and roll it back and forth vigorously. This 'feathers' it into fine threads that will catch easily. Place it over the pyramid of dust, leaving some space for a spark to hit the tinder.

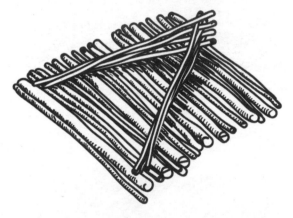

The simple 'arrow' fire lay is a tried and tested method. Place the thinnest kindling, three or four twigs at a time on top of each other on either side of the tinder to create the 'arrowhead' shape that points in the same direction the wind is blowing. The sticks should cross in interlocking layers at the tip. Build the sticks up in the same order as they were collected, from matchstick to wrist-sized, until you've gained a height of about 25 centimetres. The arrow tip where the sticks overlap should be maintained, but, as it gets higher, work the points where the two sides meet back towards the direction the wind is coming from so you end up with a covering over the tinder. Heat rises, and the idea is to capture the column of warmth that the initial flames will generate to ensure no energy is lost and the fire does not gutter.

With thorough preparation, lighting the fire should be easy. Starting it from first principles is not always essential. Indeed matches and butane lighters do the job quickly. But pride should be taken in only ever using only one rasp of the wheel or a single matchstick. It is more fulfilling, however, to create a living flame from cold materials. A knife and firesteel is best. Modern firesteel is not in fact steel, but an alloy called ferrocerium that readily gives off sparks. To use, place the tip of the firesteel in the tinder and drag the *back* edge of a knife, not the blade, down it into the fire, creating showers of sparks. Be firm and decisive with each stroke until you are sending flaring lines into the heart of the bird's nest.

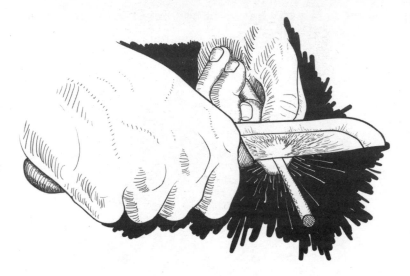

From the moment the birch catches, the world stills. Do the same. A young fire is like an eye: prod it and it will blink and close. Left alone, it will open and take in its surroundings. Sit back and watch, for this is old magic at work, a bright flame, minuscule and orange, flickering and growing. A hissing and a crackle as it spreads to the rest of the nest and the smoke thickens. Suddenly the breeze lifts and blows oxygen into the tinder and the arrow's tip is fully ablaze. After a few minutes the thermal column is throwing out heat and light across the circle of earth, igniting a whoosh of elation in its creator. Yet starting a fire is only the beginning. Mastering the element is an art form that takes practice.

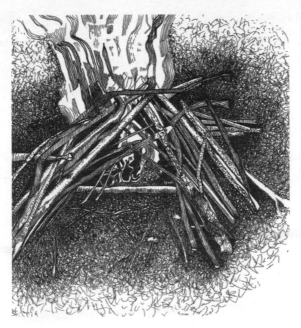

Good fire makers instinctively gather flammable natural materials whenever and wherever they occur, stuffing them in pockets close to their skin to dry. For our ancestors, fire meant the difference between warmth and light and cold and dark, between life and death. The ability to make it was always at the forefront of their minds and they picked suitable tinder where they found it, regardless of their need: sticky, amber resin found among the bark and branches of spruce and pine trees, dry grasses, the light, cottony white fluff found on rosebay willowherb and the sausage-like cattails on bulrushes. But we had walked into the forest with our pockets empty. Finding tinder had required a sharpening of our senses.

The beauty of the deciduous wood in summer is a balm to the spirit. Woodpeckers drilled holes in the trees in the distance, their knocking interspersed with melodious conversation between blue tits and robins. Our search took us under washing line trails of ivy, over patches of dog's mercury, bramble and dry ditches filled with the footprints of fallow deer. The occasional fallen birch tree meant setting to work, peeling back the bark in sheets that came away like scrolled parchment. Every now and then a brown, woody rope strong enough for Tarzan to swing on twisted its way down across our path. This was honeysuckle, a thick vine that feathers into wispy long strips, another perfect tinder. Our pockets rustled with the stuff by the time we settled on a clearing among the nettles. We constructed our platform before venturing out again to gather the kindling and fuel. Half an hour later our preparation was complete and the tinder took with just one strike of a knife down the firesteel.

The forest floor was strewn with orchids and violets bathed in the rays of afternoon sunlight that flicked intermittently through gaps in the breeze-blown canopies of oak and lime. Before us, the flames of a burgeoning fire mirrored the silky effect of wind on the sunlight in perfect synchronicity. We had spent an hour or more happily lost among the trees in search of tinder and our hard work was rewarded with the flashes of gold flaring up from the sticks. Basking in our accomplishment, the urge to lie back on our elbows and lose ourselves in the dancing flames was overpowering, but it was time to shape our fire for its next purpose.

We spread out some ash and charcoaling wood to one

side to boil a kettle of water for tea. Because we had kept the sticks long when we collected them, it was easy to take the ends that were not burning and manoeuvre the heart of our fire closer to our makeshift kitchen before laying more fuel on top. When this was glowing red, we placed four hazel logs tip-first into the centre to create a cross-shape. The 'star' or 'compass' fire, named as each log represents a cardinal point, is both low effort and fuel-efficient. Lying beside it, we watched the kaleidoscope of the tree canopies melding into one another, our peace only broken when we needed to move each log inwards as they burnt and occasionally collapsed into ash.

Throughout our evolution and until relatively recently, when electricity and gas brought modern comforts into our homes, fire was a tool, an adaptable technology that could be turned to suit a variety of needs from the personal to the industrial. Despite the distance that has grown between the developed world and this element, its versatility remains the same. Yet the closest many of us get to a fire outdoors is wrapped in scarves and clutching sparklers on 5 November. But a bonfire fuelled by petrol and towering high with pallets and broken furniture is a ritual more to do with the catharsis of torching an effigy than the enchantment of creating fire. In the warmth of our simple star we could see the traces of a skill handed down between generations over hundreds of thousands of years. Fires don't need to be big to work. To burn giant heaps of the fuel among the trees would have seemed as out of place as hearing the roar of a Ferrari. We kept our flames small and low, knowing the true secret when it comes to wood is quality over quantity.

It is a myth that all wood burns well. That is not to say each kind doesn't have a purpose. If you are trying to attract attention with a signal fire or stave off midges, smoke is best, in which case green, leafy elder with its natural insect repellent does the trick, but you wouldn't want to sit around it for long. In cold or wet conditions a bright, hot fire that flares up is essential, so split softwoods like hazel, birch, pine, fir or larch work well, even if they tend to spit and disappear quickly.

On that evening the shadows cast by the sun began to lengthen and we pulled ourselves from the mesmerising blaze to explore the surrounding area again, this time searching for bigger logs that would last the night. Through the trees the flames flicked safely, cocooned in the circle of bare earth. We didn't worry about leaving it. Deciduous woodland in Britain has a natural protection against forest fire thanks to the trees growing at respectful distances, the choking leaf litter, the green plant material and cold soil, which acts like a damp sponge. It is not the same story in evergreen or pinewoods, or near gorse bushes and heather where one stray spark may cause the ground to start smouldering and a breath of wind could then mean complete devastation.

In recent years we have seen increasing reports of such wild fire being started deliberately or because of a discarded cigarette or glass bottle refracting the sun. Instead of educating and allowing the space to make and understand it, fire is demonised; we prohibit its creation at every turn. Woods are private property, patrolled and tightly monitored. Bits of scrubland where children could once make campfires are now fenced off and barbed-wire protected. Did this authoritarian approach work with sex education? Hardly. Fire and sex, both too exciting not to explore, both too innate to repress.

Cradling hefty branches between us, it was hard not to reflect on how this distance brings another unfortunate consequence: a lack of intimacy with wood itself. Not so long ago, everyone would have recognised each tree they passed, its qualities and uses. People carefully chose their location when making fire for fear of damaging the land they depended on and created evocative rhymes to remember the burning qualities of each wood:

Beech will burn bright and clear, if the logs are kept a year.

Store for fires at Christmastide with green holly laid beside.

Chestnut is only good they say, if for years 'tis stayed away.

But ash burns green and ash burns brown, fit for a Queen with a golden crown.

Oaken logs, if dry and old, keep away the winters cold.

Poplar gives a bitter smoke, fills your eyes and makes you choke.

Elm wood burns like churchyard mould, even the very flames burn cold.

Hawthorn bakes the sweetest bread, so it is in Ireland said.

Apple wood will scent your room and pear wood smells like a flower in bloom.

But ash wood wet and ash wood dry, a King may warm his slippers by.

The gentle glow of our fire was a lighthouse in the darkening evening and we swam back through the sea of trees, birch, hazel and oak logs our life rafts. Bark stuck to our jumpers and the smell of foliage filled our noses. Soon other smells joined the wood smoke as we began to prepare an evening meal. The food was nothing out of the ordinary. Steaks – not foraged, just expertly hunted from the reduced shelf in the supermarket – alongside some boiled root vegetables. A bed of wild garlic chanced upon while scoping out fuel for the fire provided a flavoursome addition. The versatility of an open fire for cooking is surprising. Carrots, turnip and sweet potato simmered in a pan on embers left from making tea. Only a few centimetres away, the licking flames seared the steaks perfectly, crisp on the outside and bloody in the middle.

There are many theories on how our ancestors first made fire, ranging from the mundane to the implausible. Perhaps taking the flame from a tree struck by lightning? Perhaps encouraged to experiment, having discovered the delicious taste of animals trapped in forest fires? Or maybe just by happy accident, sending sparks into nearby dried twigs while making flint tools? Whether these actions came out of luck, judgement or boredom is impossible to know now but, whatever the source, the ability to control fire was a dramatic leap for early humans. The heat would help people stay warm in cold weather, enabling them to live in cooler climates and migrate or remain north in the face of encroaching glaciers. The light kept nocturnal predators at bay, reducing the need to find caves or climb up to safety. Cooking became possible, increasing the variety and availability of nutrients. Fire breaks down collagen fibres in meat into gelatin, making it less chewy and easier to digest, while cooking tubers releases far more calories. This culinary revolution may have helped bring us down from the trees to live on the ground permanently.

Natural historians now posit that more readily available calories provided the spark for further human evolution. Our jaws and teeth became gradually smaller as our diet became easier. Hunting and scrapping over a kill became less important than a safe cooking spot and the ability to recognise nutritious vegetation. Fire was the ultimate tool, but also an enchanting, hypnotic, living artwork, changing shape and form before our eyes. It was both a necessity and an inspiration.

The place of fire at the centre of the camp has been retained; it is still at the heart of many living rooms, where the business of socialising takes place. For better or worse, though, the glow of a television set is the focus point from more comfy armchairs now, taking the old role of storyteller out of the bodies of the onlookers and into the fire itself. While it brings news and entertainment that would have been inconceivable in the past, there is something that the wittering television singularly fails to deliver, which fire still brings. Fire holds your attention, certainly, and can be soporific if you are that way inclined, but while it occupies the senses with its flickering, its crackle, its warmth and scent, it offers up no message to occupy your conscious mind. It frees that part of you. It is impossible not to reflect in front of it.

The fire sheds light on the recesses of the mind. With the darkness at bay, out of sight, we also look at the faces glowing dully in the half-light. We commune with each other. We share stories to amuse and entertain, but also to build a sense of shared experiences, of connection to one another. We sing songs, often picking the ones that everyone knows and building more sense of coherence still. We cannot help but start down the road to civilisation once again, beginning to build a tribe with whoever is around the fire, cooking together, eating together, sharing our happiness and sadness. There is also something of the confessional about it. In the soft glow, people speak more freely than if they were staring into the eyes of the listeners in a bright room. It is a space to open up, punctuated only by the rustle of the natural world.

We are part of the natural world, elemental creators, part of the trees around us and the unjudging animals, but we are set apart as well. Fire defined our humanity and separation from the beasts more clearly than any other early technology. The wall of darkness at our back is the first form of the divide between 'us' and 'them'. No wonder those religions that emphasise the primacy of humanity in the world are filled with references to 'the light in the darkness', 'the fire'. Moses is visited by God through a living flame in the story of the burning bush; Buddhism saw fire as the flame of enlightenment against the darkness of ignorance; Zarathustra, credited as founder of the oldest monotheistic world religion, perceived fire as the manifestation of a higher plane and a purifier; Greek mythology talks of the titan Prometheus stealing fire from the gods. Alone in the dark woods, it is not hard to see why so much importance was attached to starting a flame that it attained a mystical significance. Every other creature, in burrow or bough, seems perfectly suited to this environment. We alone are helpless without knowledge and just as surely as we have used fire to alter our conditions of living, it has altered us in its turn.

For us this gift of fire came wrapped up with all these feelings, and as we rolled out mats and arranged our sleeping bags either side of the small flame and glowing coals, we felt warm at heart. We benefited here from a little bit of know-how. Anyone can get a noise out of a trumpet, but this is very different to playing it well. Fire is the same. The heart of our camp produced just the right amount of heat for cooking, and kept us warm while we sat almost on top of it supervising the meal. Making a fire too big is a classic mistake: you have to stand away from the inferno, and your back gets cold while your front cooks. So we had rearranged the fuel to make a line, one and a half metres long and less than 30 centimetres across, and placed a few of our largest fuel logs on the top. These would burn slowly through until morning, keeping us cosy from end to end as we slept beneath the stars.

'He who sits by the fire, thankless for the fire, is just as if he had no fire. Nothing is possessed save in appreciation, of which thankfulness is the indispensable ingredient.' W. J. Cameron's point is that in the end all we have is how the fire has made us feel. It is the perfect antidote to a culture obsessed with material possessions. By learning the skill of building a good fire, we tap into something far more profound than the act of just setting wood alight. We are closer to nature, and closer to our own nature. Our ancestors throng the dark space beyond the circle, and we draw closer to the people alongside us.

Mountains and Rivers

Build an igloo

Constructing the classic Inuit shelter may seem like something only an experienced citizen of the arctic, raised to the task, could accomplish. But with the right weather and a bit of knowledge, anyone anywhere in the world can turn snow into the most amenable building material imaginable.

The sort of equipment required can be obtained easily, a sturdy blade of some kind to cut the blocks and shape them. Eskimos use a snow knife that resembles a straight machete, the key quality being its length, 15–30 centimetres, to facilitate working with large slabs. A wood saw is a good substitute and handy to have with you given its usefulness in cutting hard-packed snow. You will also need a metre of string and it may be worth packing a plastic box so that you can still fashion sizeable bricks if the snow is powdery. Finally, find a friend. Igloos can be constructed alone, but the process is much easier and far more enjoyable with two people: a designated snow mason to cut the blocks, and a builder who will shape and place them together.

Find a flat area where snow has lain for a day or two, hardening in the wind. Testing the surface is just a matter of walking around. Snow only becomes a good building material when it has been solidified by the action of the weather, compacted and strengthened by partial thawing during the day and refreezing overnight. If you sink up to your knees then it will probably be too friable to lift wedges from intact. In which case, you'll need that box. By packing looser flakes down into the container, especially if its sides have been previously rubbed down with Vaseline to aid release, you can create the denser material needed.

Look at the ground and work out the size of igloo you want. This is up to you to decide, but don't make your circle too big; if it's your first time, then it might be best to start with a test igloo you can build entirely from the outside, something less than a metre in diameter being a good starting point. Once you are happy with the basic technique you can then move up to making one a couple of metres across, which requires one person to remain inside during the construction. Work on the proviso that a 2-metre diameter on the ground will fit two people comfortably and three at a push. An experienced Inuit can construct an igloo in forty-five minutes, but if it is your first time, somewhere between four and five hours will be a more realistic estimate.

Trace the circle using the string. Have one person hold it or tie the string to a stick driven into the snow and pull it taut. Then walk around to make the circle, which must be close to perfect or the domed structure may collapse because of uneven pressure on the base. Just as a nice smooth arch from the ground cannot easily fall, a regular dome will be much more stable.

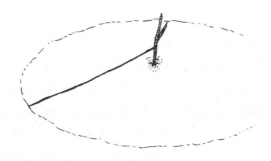

Cutting blocks is straightforward. Start with a rectangular trench that fits inside the circle you have drawn. This will also lower the floor of the igloo, giving more room inside. Extending this beyond the circular wall creates an entrance tunnel, which also acts as a cold sink, drawing chilled air down out of the sleeping area. Dig this opening so it lies leeward of the prevailing wind, ensuring a draft-free night. Using the wood saw or snow knife, slice two parallel lines through the snow, bearing in mind that the distance apart will determine the length of your slabs. For mini igloos, smaller blocks are the order of the day, but a construction a couple of metres across needs pieces between 50 and 75 centimetres in length – long enough that you make quick progress, but short enough to avoid distorting the shape of the circle. Next, cut the ends of the trench before creating the slabs themselves. Imagine you are slicing a loaf of bread. If the snow is deep enough, you should make each 'slice' about 12 to 13 centimetres thick, the height of each coming from the depth of the snow – preferably 30 centimetres or so. If the snow is not so deep, cut each slice further apart to give oblongs of the required height, the depth of the snow therefore becoming the thickness of the wall.

Lifting the first slab out can be tricky. Try cutting a handhold to the side so you can get underneath and raise the whole thing in one piece. Once you've done the first it's much easier to liberate subsequent wedges, but it's a good idea to run the saw along the underside before lifting. Of course, if you're making bricks with a box, the process is easier but you are restricted to its specific dimensions.

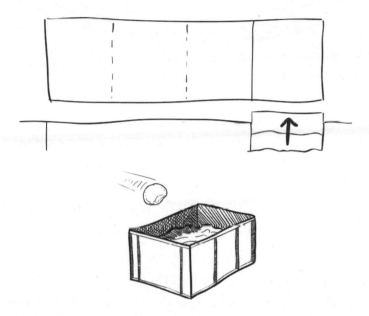

Place the first pieces along your sketched-out circle, cutting the edges at an angle so they butt together and follow the shape drawn on the ground as you go along. You will also need to cut the bottom of each piece so that they lean inwards slightly. After you arrange the first complete ring, it's time for the ingenious part. Cut an incline into the blocks that starts at ground level and runs around at least a third of the circle before it reaches the full height again. For the second layer, start adding blocks at the bottom of the ramp so the wall spirals upwards smoothly as you progress.

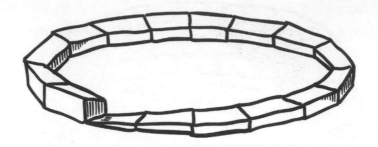

Before placing each block on the second and subsequent layers, you must keep on sloping the top of the layer beneath inwards. When you put a slab on top, it will lean towards the centre. This might seem disingenuous and likely to cause collapse, but it is in fact the key to a stable igloo. Bevelling the sides of each wedge and butting it together with the next one will hold the pieces in place as the spiral begins to form. Only the most recent block should need support against falling inwards and the more rapidly you slope inwards, the more stable it will be. The completed igloo should look like the very top of an egg, and gains its strength from the same principle. It is very difficult to crush an egg with pressure end-to-end, because bottom and top are domed. Conversely, the centre of an egg can be crushed more easily because it is flatter; if you build the walls of your igloo too straight, they will be more like the sides of an egg, and too weak.

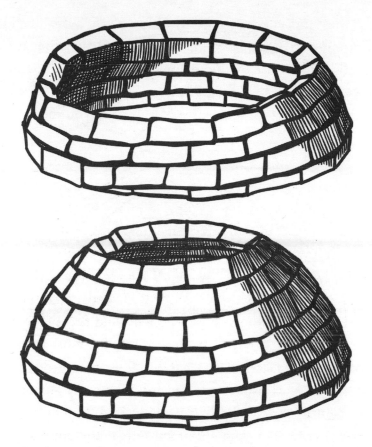

As the spiralling rings become tighter you may need to use progressively smaller elements. Cut them to fit and, if possible, overlap joins in the layer below to add strength, like in a regular brick wall. You will also find that the increasing curvature means the bottom of a flat block won't sit snugly on top: each must be given a slightly curved base to fit.

The action for shaping slabs should be rapid back-and-forth strokes. Do this between two adjacent wedges to slice irregularities off both, and then push them together and check the fit. If they're not quite flush, continue to trim. The angle of every cut, whether it's bevelling to ensure a good fit or steepening the slope of the latest ring, should lead back towards a point at the centre of the igloo: the centre of the circle you drew on the ground.

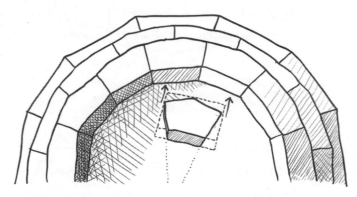

Practice is key, but with each round being laid and the hemisphere taking shape, the sense of achievement increases a thousandfold, driving the determination to finish even more. Eventually, the person on the inside will be nearing the point of placing the keystone. This is the final wedge in the spiral, which should be at the centre of the dome. Because of the spiral, the hole in the top will likely be in a comma shape rather than a circle, so as you complete the final layer you should carve a penultimate piece to leave a more regular polygonal hole. This can be filled with a large slab slid out from the inside, and then cut to shape as it is lowered back into place.

Just as someone painting a floor finds himself or herself backed into a corner, the igloo builder should now be blocked inside. Cut an exit hole over the cold sink trench, before filling any gaps in the exterior of the igloo with loose snow. This should harden as it is exposed to any wind or cold weather. Finally, make a couple of small holes near the top of the igloo for ventilation. You can use a spare block to seal the doorway if spending the night.

Air pockets within the snow mean it is a fantastic insulator and, once inside, the interior of a finished igloo is like its own world. Out of the wind, with a roll mat and a decent sleeping bag, it is warm enough to sleep, ranging between 7° and 16° Celsius inside when heated by body warmth alone. The walls muffle any exterior noise, creating a unique sense of peace and calm, the greenish-yellow and blue luminescence of the changing sunlight through the blocks adding a beautiful ambience. This ethereal quality of being snugly sealed inside as wind howls around is unforgettable.

Our first attempt to build an igloo was in the Alps. Snow had fallen consistently for a few days beforehand, and temperatures plummeted overnight. As friends grabbed their skis to take to the slopes, muttering that our plans were 'too much like hard work', we hiked out of town in the late morning sun, up valley sides scattered with pines.

In the shadow of a ridge we drew our circle. We had started small to test the principle, just less than a metre, but we quickly hit a snag. While it was perfectly possible to cut into the powdery snow with a saw, nothing survived being picked up, let alone the rigours of shaping and positioning. It was like trying to make bricks from dry sand. Pausing for thought and a quick bite, the solution struck us. The tough plastic container for our packed lunch was an ideal brick-like mould and could easily withstand being rammed with snow to make the slabs for a small dome.

Laying down the first few rounds was simple enough, but by the third row we were growing a little nervous: surely we would reach a point where the blocks would topple inwards? How could two of us hope to support the dome from the outside until the keystone was laid? To our surprise, however, rather than falling inwards, we placed a piece of the fourth layer and the wall beneath collapsed *outwards*, leaving a sizeable breach. The rest of the structure stayed intact, so we decided to rebuild the rupture from the ground up. Having done so, we continued around again, only for the same point to collapse under the fifth circle. By this time, the shadows were lengthening and the temperature dropping. Confused and downhearted, we decided, like British Rail, to blame the 'wrong kind of snow' and retraced our steps back to the chalet, clapping our gloved hands under our armpits and stamping our feet to try and keep warm.

That evening by the fire we discussed why we had failed, both agreeing the error was our fear of having the walls collapse inwards. Early layers had been too vertical. When the arch began to form above them, they were pushed out by its weight. This is a key lesson for dealing with the snow: trust is everything. You must trust the knowledge you have learned. Natives of these extreme conditions stick to their traditional methods to keep them safe.

We awoke to find we had both experienced vivid dreams during the night. These were dreams filled with the glaring light and memories of the sharp bite of snow on exposed skin. Having spent most of the day concentrating intently on such an unusual skill as whittling blocks into shape had triggered something fundamental in our brains. We had become obsessed with this new knowledge, and were clearly reliving our mistakes as we slept: visions of igloos that fell again and again no matter how we built them up had filled our sleep, along with the distinctive sound of a knife slashing through the snow, always followed by a gentle crunching as the cut blocks came together again, every surface glaring mercilessly under the sun.

As humans we are designed to acquire new skills. Endorphins are released to give us pleasure when we succeed at understanding a new task. The ability to soak up such basic skills as building a shelter from whatever is to hand is precisely why our species survived to become what it is today. So many modern skills are divorced from this basic relationship between learning ability and surviving more effectively. Good enough is, all too frequently, just good enough. We can survive doing very little. Yet for the people living beyond the northern tree line, the relationship between work and success was brutally direct and exacting. Out on the sea ice, hunters need to know how to build igloos quickly and effectively, how to harness the element that will kill them otherwise. At these extremes there is an understanding of a duality in nature, that it is both a destructive and a constructive force. This balance between what they could take from nature and the price it would exact in return loomed large in the consciousness of the Inuit. It is captured in their old saying: 'The great peril of our existence lies in the fact that our diet consists entirely of souls'.

Perhaps we had failed to understand the depth of this relationship with the harshest conditions. We didn't trust in the technique because we weren't subject to the same repercussions. We were still able to gorge on the rich melted cheese and white wine of a fondue that evening despite our inadequacy on the mountain. Our second attempt saw us both firmly determined to succeed. We travelled higher into the mountains in search of tougher snow, picking a spot off-piste, over-watched by the summit of Mont Blanc. We worked from the early morning, having risen before dawn, and the sun was still low behind mountains to the south and east as we drew out a circle and began to cut the first trench. It was much colder work than the relatively balmy −1° Celsius implied, and we set to with alacrity to keep ourselves warm. By the time the second ring had been set in place, the bleakness of the unending snowy blue was fading. Mountains opposite were bathed in golden sunlight, and the contrast between their fiery glory and the twilight blue in which we worked made it seem as though our own location had, if anything, darkened as the sun rose.

Our efforts drew the attention of early skiers, inquisitive couples watching how we tackled the snow. The distinctive green and white uniforms of a French army mountain regiment on skiing practice also slid to a standstill nearby. We had heard the army had been building quinzhees here a few days before. These are more rudimentary snow shelters constructed by piling up a mound of snow and then tunnelling into it, using 30-centimetre sticks driven into the top and sides, like a balding hedgehog, to gauge the thickness of the walls and judge when to stop digging. They paused to shake hands and marvel at the igloo's construction as its distinctive form emerged from the endless, featureless drifts.

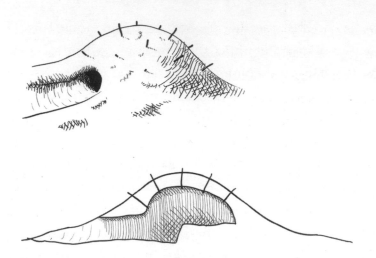

Each successive pass around the curving structure brought further changes in the light. We broke for rest and to consume some small, sharp apples that had almost frozen in the bag and turned into a refreshing, sour sorbet in our mouths. The sun hit the snow bank 50 metres from us. We were bathed in reflected light, giving the igloo itself and the surrounding remnants of our quarrying a surreal quality. Their shadows were being driven in the opposite direction to everything else we could see.

By starting the arc inwards from the very first round, we avoided the outward topple of our first attempt. The slight taper to each block meant that, as gravity pulled it inwards, it abutted its neighbour and was held in place. There is a very quick feedback loop when building an igloo. Each block falls down or stays. You are continually learning and seeing the results of your work, even when you fail. It has an addictive quality, akin to a video game. When we play games, receptors in the brain are stimulated by every incremental success and the hit of pleasure when a block fits more neatly than the last works in exactly the same way. Each layer above the ground is a new high score, and a new level to beat. It's Tetris on a grand scale.

In her book *Reality is Broken*, Jane McGonigal reveals the alarming fact that players of the online fantasy *World of Warcraft* have chalked up almost 6 million years of collective gaming. It is strange to think that people have collectively spent more time than human evolution sitting in front of screens performing repetitive tasks in a virtual world without any tangible benefit in reality. However, the action of building an igloo, arguably just as pointless in the modern world, gives you an insight into why this might be. Both activities push all the buttons for making us happy.

Games involve clearly defined but challenging tasks. They offer the hope of success and, following enough work, the experience of it. These qualities are present in the difficult task of igloo building. We all know the sense of pleasure that comes from having everything in its right place and, for us, seeing each fashioned block interlocking with its fellow as the walls rose higher and higher was truly joyous. It combined all the pride of a well-architected plan coming together with the immediate satisfaction of improving at our craft, as forming each layer we became quicker and more accurate. This was certainly the 'satisfying work' that McGonigal talks about; we knew it was challenging from our previous failure, but we had every hope of succeeding.

Connecting with others imbues gaming with a shared sense of meaning because of the sheer number of people involved. In the case of *World of Warcraft* it's 12 million, larger than the populations of Greece, Cuba or Portugal. A community inhabiting the same virtual space perhaps generates feelings similar to patriotism. There isn't a million-strong community of igloo-builders around the world today, but creating a shelter in the snow hardwires us into ancient traditions and instincts that bind humanity across the aeons. As you weatherproof the exterior of an igloo, rubbing snow into the cracks, you become aware that your hands are following movements made by many men and women who have melted away over time.

Game makers talk about the addictive nature of 'fiero', an Italian word for fire-like pride, which they use specifically to describe the sudden rush of joy that comes from beating the odds. As we progressed, we could feel the same sense of anticipation building towards it.

We laboured on until, as time came to prepare the keystone, the sun crested the southern hilltop. Matching the angle of the slope almost exactly, the light gave the snow an eerie quality, hitting it almost perfectly edge-on, leaving it darker than the brightly lit trees and scintillating with every movement of our eyes. Each tiny ridge and rivulet in the landscape was a subtle or a sudden gradient from grey-blue to blinding white.

Naturalist Joseph Wood Krutch remarked, 'The snow itself is lonely or, if you prefer, self-sufficient. There is no other time when the whole world seems composed of one thing and one thing only.' This is a remarkable contrast to the patchwork of fields, forests, lakes, rivers and buildings that we usually see covering the land, and on a morning where snow has fallen overnight you can tell from the quality of the light creeping through the curtains, even before going to the window, that a very different world awaits you outside. By spending time in a single spot you can draw closer to the incredible alien beauty of this white landscape, superimposed on the familiar.

It would not occur to most of us to simply sit and watch the progression of the sun over a snowy hill for six hours, but the concentration and exertion required to build an igloo kept us there. This is not to say that time passed without us realising. Indeed, every second of labouring, cutting, lifting, placing and shaping was keenly felt. The painful chill on the wrist where the hem of a glove and the sleeve of a coat was failing to meet, or a complaint from the small of your back, kept us very much present. The rhythm of the tasks, moving from assemblage to block building, pausing every hour or so for a short rest and some ice-cold water, seemed to form a jigsaw puzzle in time as self-supporting as the dome itself. It would not have been possible to be bored.

This is a state American psychologist Csikszentmihalyi described as 'flow': 'the satisfying, exhilarating feeling of creative accomplishment and heightened functioning'. In truth, many of the things we may think of as likely to make us happier and more relaxed, from achieving wealth, popularity or fame to watching television and shopping, have actually been shown to have little effect on our general mood, or even to have a negative impact. In contrast, autotelic activities, where the rewards come from our own efforts rather than externally, have been shown to yield a sense of self-worth and optimism. We were working hard all day making our igloo, having risen at an ungodly hour, yet when we put our feet up late that evening the sense of relaxation and accomplishment was far more complete and wholesome than if we had spent the day at a less taxing activity.

The wonderful thing about snow is that it is a material anyone can work with. Since mastering the technique, we have built igloos of varying sizes in the Scottish Highlands, on the Yorkshire Moors, and even in London. When snow falls, people anywhere immediately feel the urge to do things with it. Anyone who has built a snowman or engaged in a snowball fight knows this very well. These are some of the most basic instincts of creation and play: fashioning a simulacrum of ourselves, mock battle, and building a den. All the same principles used in constructing a building of stone or brick are to be found in igloo building. We quarry our materials, shape them to our needs, and lay them according to our plans. From time to time we even found ourselves wedging in off-cuts to reinforce the structure, like building a drystone wall, and the final result can be as perfect a half-sphere as any church dome. Yet because of snow's pliable nature, all of this can take place in a matter of hours. In today's world of specialists, few of us get the chance to build a dwelling from scratch. There are regulations and permissions to be sought. Even architects and master builders are constrained to be one part of a larger process. Snow turns the entire world into a single thing, and all of us into artists, warriors and masons.

This is also about the conquering of a wild and dangerous element. Snow is a defining feature of winter. We live in a country where it sometimes seems to stop everything, and being able to master it sets a limit on its power over us. Turning it from a danger or an annoyance into a fabulous structure is liberating.

Like the blossom on trees, perhaps it is the ephemeral nature of this structure that makes it so special. Built in a garden, an igloo may remain as a barometer for the season. As it gradually thaws, we know spring is around the corner, the season of new life, when newer, natural structures will emerge from the frozen ground to take its place.

It is said that you can't find happiness: you have to make it. Something that is easily achieved can feel devoid of meaning, but our failure the day before, combined with an admiring audience watching the second attempt, had made building a finished igloo on that mountainside a challenge we desperately needed to meet. When the keystone was down, and our entrance tunnel cut, we felt ourselves lords of this domain. We threw our arms up, sharing a surge of 'fiero'; an unforgettable fiery pride in the icy landscape.

Catch a fish

Magazines and television shows dedicated to fishing may lead you to believe it is an exclusive sport, a pastime for the fully kitted. Yet the principle of fishing couldn't be simpler: conceal a hook with bait, drop it into the water, and wait for a fish to bite it. With only a little effort and a couple of pounds spent on shop-bought items, basic rod and tackle can be fashioned that is every bit as effective as expensive equipment.

A simple fishing pole is best made from a dead sapling that is still standing and is as straight, tall and thin as you can find. Dead saplings will have dried out and be lighter than living ones and, unlike fallen wood, are less likely to be rotten. Coppiced hazel and ash woods are the most fertile hunting grounds. Look amid groups of living saplings for the thin and leafless that stand rigid among their fellows, the ideal being at most 5 centimetres in diameter and at least 2 metres high. Once found, snap or saw it as close to the base as you can and remove any twigs that branch off. The pole should have the rigidity of dead wood, still with a little flex towards the thin end, but the key is its length and the longer the better. Pole fishing allows the angler to lower bait in specific areas, using the rod's length to reach the best 'swims' rather than casting a line, so it is worth taking the time to look for a sapling that will span as much of the stretch of water you intend to fish as possible. Bear in mind that the odd kink here and there doesn't matter provided the overall line of the thin trunk is fairly even.

If getting hold of a sapling is difficult, you can substitute other similarly shaped material of the right length: an old curtain rod, perhaps, or long broom handle. Bamboo cane is particularly good as it has natural flexibility, weighs relatively little and is very cheap. Choose the longest canes you can and bind sections together with string or cord until you reach a total length of between 2 and 4 metres.

To lash them, overlap at least a quarter of the canes and tie a clove hitch around both near the end of the section of cane you are attaching. Tie this knot by wrapping the cord around both sections with the end passing below the standing part as you come back around to the front. Make another turn around both sections before pushing the end through the new loop you have just created and pull tight. Then lash with eight to ten turns round both sections to hold them together and finish with another clove hitch. You can strengthen this join by adding a second identical lashing higher up.

With rod complete, you need a float. Find a feather that measures between 25 and 30 centimetres. The easiest thing is to keep an eye out whenever you are in the outdoors and build up a collection at home that you can draw upon. Check around riverbanks as those from a goose or swan make ideal fishing floats, having big air chambers where the feather meets the follicle. Feathers can decay if on the ground too long so avoid any that feel soft or spongy or those that have been out in the wet for any length of time.

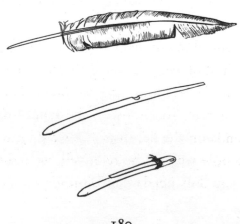

Trim the flights off by running the blade of a knife up each side from the bottom to the tip. Alternatively, you can find the membrane that attaches the feathers to the quill by pulling the softer stuff at the top apart. Get your fingernail underneath and peel down the length of the feather like removing a sticking plaster. Take care as you near the bottom, however, not to tear a hole in the air chamber as the integrity of this section will give the float its buoyancy in the water. Next, cut the remaining feather down to about 15 centimetres, trimming away the tapering top end. Hold the quill up to the light and you should be able to see where the air chamber turns into the thicker chalky 'rachis' or main shaft. Some 3 or 4 centimetres along from the end you just cut, and before it turns into the air chamber, hollow out a groove a centimetre wide in the rachis, being careful not to work all the way through. Bend the shorter end over on itself so the groove forms an 'eye' where it folds. If you can't see a hole, cut away some more of the rachis around it until you can. Now tie the folded end down using fishing line, string or any cordage to hand.

Nylon monofilament fishing line, a hook and two BB-sized split-shot weights cost little and can be bought in any tackle or outdoor sports shops. Pole fishing doesn't use a reel, so choosing the length of line to attach depends on the depth of the water you are fishing in. The pole tip will be relatively near the water's surface, so you only need to account for a maximum of a metre of line up to the float and then whatever depth below it you estimate will have the bait sitting at around 7 to 10 centimetres from the bottom. This obviously varies from location to location so it may be best to set the rod by the water where you can make an informed assessment.

When you have found your fishing spot, cut a V-shaped notch at the tip of the rod and tie your fishing line around the middle to prevent any slippage. Thread the other end of the line through the eye of the feather float, pull it through, and thread it again in the same direction. The float will now be in a loop, which will allow you to move its position freely should you need to adjust the depth you are fishing at. Attach a weight just below the float and squeeze it closed on the line with a pair of pliers or, at a push, your teeth. Add another one or two (depending on the depth of the water) between the float and the end of the line and, finally, tie on a hook using the fisherman's favourite, a half-blood knot. This is an easy and reliable fastening. Just thread the line through the hook's eye twice to create a loop, wrap it four or five times back around the line and feed the end back through the initial loop. With your whole rig in place, avoid tangles in transit by pulling the hook down the length of the rod until the line is taut and cutting another notch at the place it reaches. You can then secure the hook to this and transport the rod safely.

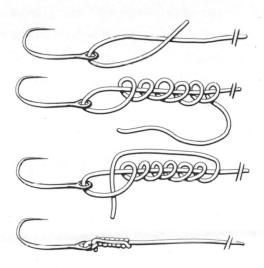

There is a sense of pride in carrying a homemade rod to the water's edge. As any fisherman will tell you the rod is a conduit for the angler's skills and knowledge, an extension of your self that allows you to commune with the water. The more personal it is, the closer you get.

The river wound its way through the terrain like a ribbon. From the distance it flowed long and slow, appearing deceptively still but with the underlying muscular strength of movement. The bright spring morning flashed over its surface and it gleamed as if polished. Wading through the grass, comfrey and knee-high nettles, we negotiated a crumbling bank, doubling our hazel rods as walking sticks, and dropped down to the edge. The water's coldness was tangible, a fridge door open in a warm kitchen. It felt as though the last of winter was being drawn from the landscape, leaving in its place the thick, green smell of new life, which hung draped across the young leaves of the riverside aspen, horse chestnut and willow. In the bosom of the flow, the fresh water was imperceptibly swift, a clear, crystal curve folding into itself, sweeping over shallower stretches, only to shatter on the rocks around the bend. At other spots the water was still and translucent, beef-stock brown and ruffled only by a gentle eddy bobbing back upstream. Such is the nature of wild bodies of water. They are so many things at once: complex, mysterious, fascinating and enchanting, like a person.

An angler cannot help but become a naturalist. The river teaches you where to site your rod, as long as you are prepared to learn its language. Alternating between dropping our eyes to the surface and standing to survey the scene, we began to see the river's nuances. They opened up before us like a map. Here the sunlight picked out the waving fingers of luminescent weed that would snare our lines. There the water pulled through the rocks at speeds too fast for our floats.

In the stiller scene of a lake, canal or pond, there is less danger of bait getting dragged uselessly up to the surface by any current. But this water was a different animal, alive with character and a rippling, gurgling sound.

Perhaps our best bet lay in the quiet of the eddy? These forgotten pools were positioned off the main flow like trackside pit stops, acting as natural collection points for the detritus and delights that washed downstream. Clouds of brown trout fry danced away from our reflections as we crept along the bank to reach them. This was a good sign. The morning sun was warming the water on the margins of the main flow and creating a comfortable temperature for fish to feed. Ducking under low boughs and over patches of bramble we came to a beech tree in the process of succumbing branch-by-branch to the pull of the river. On its lee side lay a good stretch of slack water, stout-coloured and still. Fish congregate in places of safety and its many submerged branches and roots offered dark caves and hidey-holes aplenty. No sooner had we settled than the unmistakable *schlop* of a rising trout broke the silence as if to commend our choice. We retrieved our bait from a plastic lunch box, two purpley-pink earthworms dug fresh from the adjoining meadow. Threading the body of the worms along the hooks to disguise the metal, we wedged the rods into position between rocks and roots only centimetres above the water's surface, the hazel poles indistinguishable from the overhanging branches kissing the water. The feather floats trembled in slow circles in the eddy wash 3 metres out from the bank, assuring us that our worms were clear of the murky bottom. Among the bankside armies of fern and dock, we hunkered down to wait.

Fishing requires total silence and stillness. Amid this calm, concealed from view in tall vegetation, everything slows. Time starts to slip away downstream. Whether it is seconds, minutes or hours passing, we can't be sure. Eyes are drawn to the rhythm of the float; we are at the whim of the river's time. It is as though our very fingers are brushing the surface. Through the feather float we watch the flow. Feel the flow, even. Breathing becomes deeper, the heart rate slows, the muscles relax and the mind empties, following only that singular object through every gentle twist and bubbling ripple. Fishing is meditation, even if we don't realise it.

As early as 1653, in his seminal and still much-loved fishing tome *The Compleat Angler*, Izaak Walton said as much: 'Rivers and the inhabitants of the watery element were made for wise men to contemplate, and fools to pass by without consideration.' Such contemplation can be easy to dismiss and difficult to access without a reason for staying. Most of us will have walked past or perhaps picnicked by a river at some point, but it is rare to remain for any longer than an hour focused exclusively on the water. Fishing legitimises the stay; it gives an excuse to be there. It is a prop for the idler that vindicates a day spent staring into the natural world, repaying patience with a journey of the imagination down the rod and line into the dark depths. It takes us out of ourselves.

We gazed at ripples forming around the floats and as tiny bubbles broke the surface; each uncharacteristic dip and bob pulled us further under. Was it the changes of the river's flow or a fish circling, nosing up to the bait and darting away? What did the fish look like? Which direction was it coming from? We were tracing the movements we imagined happening below. If we half shut our eyes and allowed our peripheral vision to take over, it felt as though we could see through the dark and distinguish the outlines of bodies moving through the water. In this state, time and space merged as upstream became 'the future', downstream 'the past', the present moment constantly reforming in front of us. We had entered a state Kant described as 'Interesselosigkeit' or 'disinterested'. This is something very different from 'uninterested'. The conscious, analytical mind relaxes and fades in the incoming sensations, lost in the moment. Kant wrote of the 'free play' of imagination and understanding when observing art. He cited the pleasure of pure contemplation, in which there is no effort needed to do anything, no requirement to act, nothing except to enjoy the moment unfurling before you. We felt the same gazing on nature's ever-changing canvas.

Clouds filtered a reluctant sun and common blue-tailed male damselflies appeared to dance where rays lit the more brackish-brown water. Something flashed out of a tennis ball-sized hole and plopped into the river, a water vole perhaps, but too fast for our eyes to distinguish. We all know how noisy, distracting and relentless a city can be, but we tend to associate the great outdoors with quiet. Our silence, one we need to reserve when fishing, revealed a soundscape just as lively. Against the constant, calming rush of water and birdsong, trout slapped intermittently against the surface, tantalisingly close to our floats but apparently more interested in displaying their talent for telling the difference between insects and early blossom floating in the current. Ducks fussed and marshalled unruly broods of ducklings away from the scarecrow shadow of a grey heron overhead, their quacks drowned out by its rasping, tubular croak. Somewhere unseen, lambs bleated and the occasional rustle of foliage behind us betrayed other animals rummaging through tunnels in the undergrowth.

Spending time by a river is, in a way, like watching a road at rush hour. The natural world travels on it, in it and around it, going to work or returning home, the busy chirps and calls are the horns of a highway cutting through the green landscape. Naturalist and author J. A. Baker described humans as having a 'hoop of red-hot iron, a hundred yards across, that sears away all life' and it is true – we do scare away nature without realising. We presume an area is absent of life after a few moments' observation and move away. But by remaining angler-still, this glowing shackle cools and contracts. That day we saw and heard nature everywhere.

As the day sloped into late afternoon the river kept up its show, with an occasional change in acts. Moorhen and Canada geese drifted past, performing hilarious routines as they tried to teach their scraggly young the ways of the water. When they gave up and paddled away, the chicks suddenly cottoned on and scrambled after their wake like a string of fluffy sausages. From time to time we lifted our hazel rods to check the bait, only to find it had all too often been sneaked away and we needed to root around for a fresh worm or little slug.

The entrance of the mayfly signalled the approaching curtain of evening. In clouds they swarmed over the river, some floundering to become a trout's supper, others settling on our heads and arms. To them, we were perhaps strange vegetation under the pinking sky. We had taken root in the banks, but with our rods still empty, our sandwiches exhausted and dark gathering, we called it a night.

Even if you catch nothing, a day fishing is far from wasted. After all, with 4 million Britons citing fishing as their favourite pastime, stocks would soon be exhausted if the catch were the only purpose. Our hands were cracked with dried mud and boots squished with water, but it was a small price to pay to experience the powerful, transformative effect of the river. This is surely the angler's real addiction: establishing a place in the landscape, finding somewhere to return to through the seasons, through the years, a bolthole to escape to. Once this physical retreat has been established, the mental consolation it provides extends beyond its borders. Stressed on a Friday afternoon, with work mounting and deadlines looming, just the thought of retreating to the river the following day is a refreshing vision that alleviates the pressure. There is a realm in our minds where the river runs endlessly.

Although we now tend to think of angling squarely as a sport, in ancient times, there was of course no such luxury. Every way early man could snare freshwater and saltwater fish in large numbers was utilised; the most effective being indiscriminate clutches of nets or woven baskets. In his 1921 book *Fishing from Earliest Times*, William Radcliffe suggests one reason for the shift in mentality may have been the development of the more skilful use of rod and bait. The history of where and when these methods were first employed is somewhat hazy, but archaeologists have discovered fishing hooks dating back 20,000 years. The Egyptians were certainly using what we might recognise as prototype rods 2,000 years ago, immortalising them in tomb paintings found in Thebes. References to this form of catching fish can also be found in the poetry of Homer and the Bible; however, it is in fourth-century Chinese writing that we find the first clear allusion to angling as a distinct and restorative sport. Radcliffe notes: 'The Emperors were keen all-round sportsmen, but especially zealous disciples of the craft of Angling. Like all good fishermen, they rejoiced in having themselves or sharing with their friends a good day.'

Regardless of this noble pedigree, the sport spans class divides and remains a great leveller to this day. From troubled teenagers to country squires, all are equal in the eyes of a fish. Importantly, no matter what our background, different landscapes enable us to think in different ways; they define how we feel. Rivers have been a particularly powerful terrain in this respect throughout human history.

Our first day had been filled with delight but empty of fish. A postmortem was inevitable. Though the trout were plentiful enough, they had seemed only interested in flies. A good angler adapts. If the menu wasn't tempting to the epicurists of the main river, we needed to change location. As morning broke, we strolled to what we suspected to be another hotspot, the confluence of two rivers, and set the rods either side of a tree stump close to the mouth of the smaller feeder flow. Held in position by roots and stuck fast into the bank, we moved some metres away to leave the fish in peace. Izaak Walton praised the 'dead' rod tactic as 'like putting money to use; for they both work for the owners when they do nothing'. Again, the floats sat in the circling eddy, but this time a leaden sky kept the flies away. Nothing floated down and nothing rose to the surface. We hoped the appetite of the travellers on this meandering B-road of a brook would be different, that the fish would be inclined to try something meatier on a cold day.

It's surprising what else you find to do when just sitting on the riverbank. Our fingers began to twitch and we idly pulled away at surrounding stems and grasses, twisting them into shapes. Soon this progressed into experimenting with the tensile strength of the fibres pulled off plants and talk of making rudimentary cordage. Nettles might seem an unthinkable choice, but we found they are by far the toughest. The old adage is also true: grasp them firmly and drag up the leaves and stem and you can strip them without injury as the stinging hairs are only on the surface of the leaves. Well, with relatively few stings at least – mind over matter is important here, or a good pair of gloves. Using the wooden handle of a knife, the stems can be flattened before breaking the hard inner core and removing it to leave the outer cladding: long strips of nettle fibre. Turning either end of a 2 millimetre-wide fibre in opposite directions, the midpoint naturally twists back on itself to form a loop. Holding this loop between the thumb and forefinger leaves two strands to play with. Winding these in the same direction, but turning the loop in the other, makes a strong, thin twine. Experimenting with getting these as long as possible, it dawned on us that something similar attached to bone hooks could have been used as fishing line perhaps on this, our very river, thousands of years ago.

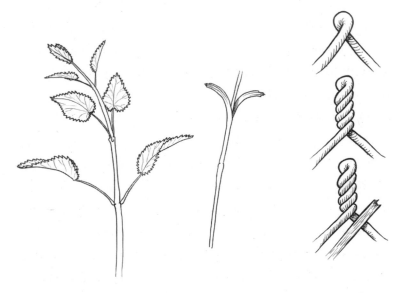

The movement of the rod tip was so unexpected we both stared at it for a moment before reacting. The hazel jumped again and we dived through the grass. A flash of silver near the surface, a flapping jolt and the sapling flexed as we lifted our catch from the water. Only 10 or 11 centimetres long, the young wild brown trout seemed as big as the white whale in our eyes and we quickly wet our hands and removed the hook from the corner of its mouth. Under his russet flanks and gold spots, a slow heartbeat, surprisingly powerful in the palm. We looked into its gazing, unblinking eye. We had done it. From scratch, we had made something that had caught a fish. A second later we lowered it gently into the river and, with a flick of its tail and a splash, it was gone.

Landing and holding our trout brought an important and immediate connection. Below the surface, our rivers, lakes and ponds are complex and fascinating societies. From the pike, to the rudd, perch and roach, the graceful grayling and many a humble minnow, dynasties exist in these hidden worlds. Fishing with a rod and line requires you to understand them, to learn each quarry's habits and home, creating in us a greater sense of their value and importance. This empathy may impress on the angler other rhythms. Fish live in harmony with the water cycle, with precipitation, evaporation and transpiration. As summer days shorten and autumn rains run freely into the rivers again, the high water sparks in salmon and migratory sea trout an innate urge to seek out native pools and spawning riffles. Taking to the banks to catch them, anglers too are integrating with these greater cycles. How the river is reborn after the dry summer influences how the fish behave, which dictates fishing seasons and ultimately the anglers' recreational time as surely as if the fish themselves had written it in the fisherman's diary.

We are often encouraged to think of life in linear terms. We are born, we live and we die. We start a job and get promoted upwards, and then retire. Job interviews ask where we see ourselves in five years, presuming the line advances in a single direction, but before our species began to pin down a linear chronology humans measured themselves and thought in terms of the cycles apparent in nature. It is in the phrases we still use in everyday language: 'turn over a new leaf', 'a new dawn'. We noted the waxing and waning of the moon, the passing of the seasons. The age-old fertility symbols of spring, the egg, the rabbit, all signified rebirth and renewal with all the possibilities they bring. Our need to be a part of this revival still manifests itself in everything from our desire to have a night on the town at the end of the week to a holiday in the sun to recharge our batteries: we feel a need to be reinvigorated. The philosopher A. C. Grayling cites this as the reason we place such importance on recreational activities in life – that they are the metaphorical re-creating of ourselves. When fishing, each cast or re-baiting of the rod is a new beginning. The river doesn't seem to change shape in a day, but the water flowing past is different to the water that moved across our vision a second before. Each breath of wind sheds a fresh batch of blossom on to its surface that is transported away. We leave the river a different person from the one who arrived, attuned to its rhythms, refreshed.

The stream we fish runs parallel to our stream of consciousness and the parallels may imbue in us a philosophical disposition. A river never fights an uphill battle in a route to the sea. When it runs into obstacles it pushes back those that it can or finds another way around. So often we butt against things when really we should be taking a step back, asking ourselves if there is an easier way to get where we are going. Flowing forward when the way is clear, keeping a gentle pressure when the way is blocked, water finds a route in the end.

Fishing had taught us the importance of going with the flow. Some days the fish will bite, some days they won't. Sitting on the bank or waist-deep in the water in waders, we are spectators to the beautiful and ever changing in nature and we are reminded that we are ever changing too. Just as you can never truly fish the same spot twice, there is no way back upstream for us. We learn to live each moment.

Dam a stream

With the possible exception of a bucket, everything needed to build a dam can be found in and around most streams. With no other preparation required, spend some time finding the right location. The many small tributaries to bigger rivers are best. Choose a quiet, free-flowing, pebbly stream measuring somewhere between 1 and 3 metres in width and reaching no higher than the top of your knee at its deepest part. Look to site your dam at the narrow points in the stream that have the greatest wealth of branches, stones, loose river rock and mud. This will be your building material, so the more stuff close to hand, the better. Walk up and down the area scanning for choke points, paying attention to where the water weaves its way around rocks and through protruding tree roots. In many cases, debris accumulates in such spots. Take a cue from nature; raid these caches for their material and even consider the obstacles as a basic foundation for your dam.

When choosing a spot, bear in mind that the deeper gullies of the watercourse might seem like harder work, but increased depth means a gentler flow, making the dam more stable while being built. Conversely, shallow rapids may look easier, but the strength of the current is harder to divert and, unless you have some very large foundations, each barrier you try to put down may be washed away before you can place the next layer.

Damming is about slowing, diverting and controlling a stream to create a 'head' of deeper, calmer water, rather than stopping the flow completely. A successful dam will have a barricade running across the majority of the stream, which diverts the water flow down a narrow discharge route to one side. With the weight of water suddenly being forced down a much smaller channel, the main body will slow considerably and create a pool upstream of the dam for you to play with.

The discharge route for the water to flow through is essential to avoid flooding and even the largest industrial barricades employ such channels for run-off. Again, use any natural obstacles such as rocks projecting above the surface and mentally apportion the width of the watercourse between your proposed dam and the channel for the flow of the stream to divert through. A good ratio to aim for is three-quarters of the stream for the dam and one-quarter for the channel.

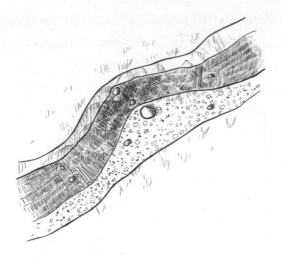

Once a suitable place is found, start from the bank and use the shallows to your advantage. Lay down a few sturdy branches on top of one another across the stream to provide structural strength to the barrier. Each one needs to span the width of the proposed dam in one piece, and this initial wall must break the surface or otherwise anything you pile on top will get washed away. It's a good idea to brace the branches against a large rock at either end so the flow of the stream holds them stationary without any additional work.

Next prop broad, flat rocks picked from the upstream side of the dam (this will deepen the bottom of the pool) and sit them vertically against this frame to fill the cross-section as quickly as possible. Towards the middle or end of the dam you may need to add two or three layers balanced on top of one another as the depth will be greater. These stones will not dam the stream to any great extent as the cracks between them will be sizeable, but you will start to see quicker spurts running around them to compensate for the impediment. Now it's time for some not-so-dry stone walling. Pick smaller pebbles, again from the upstream side of the dam to deepen the pool, and place them between and against your rows of larger rocks. Bulkier stones provide good support nearer the base. Use these to build up the foundations before working up the wall, plugging gaps as you see them. As you shore up the structure, the river should gradually develop a height difference of a good few centimetres between the front and rear of the dam and flow much more powerfully through the run-off channel. The final layer is handfuls or bucketfuls of tiny pebbles, sand and silt applied to the upstream side and top of the dam, making sure you plaster over any holes to get a complete covering. As the stream's flow and gravity takes each fine load, it should be caught in any small cracks, making a seal. If you find the water just carries the material away down the discharge route, reduce the gaps further with larger rocks or try applying another bucketful. It may be that the first provided enough additional surface area for a second attempt to stick.

When finished, stand back and study your work. Where the water previously ran at an uninterrupted pace, the dam should resemble a stony bank or levee jutting out at 90° to the shore and across three-quarters of the stream's total width. This should be holding back a noticeably raised head of water, a pool that almost submerges the upstream side of the dam. With the water flow diverted down the discharge channel, the downstream side of the dam will, in contrast, be lying exposed.

The first dam either of us had built since childhood was an impromptu feat of engineering. We had set out on a June morning to stroll along a brimming brook, one of the many tributaries of the River Teifi in Wales. Unexpectedly, the sun sat unchallenged in a cloudless sky. Each step seemed to drive the temperature up a degree and, after a few miles of draining our water supplies, we headed for the shelter offered by a gnarled willow in order to rest. The arch of its branches reached down from the opposite bank and shaded the stream like a parasol, creating a pastoral scene from the brush of a romantic landscape artist. On the flattened curve, the full, clear water trembled over brown boulders and half-submerged rocks like an overfilled glass. Taking care not to let the flow rush over the tops of our walking boots, we crossed to its inner edge and out of the glare of the sun. Here, the current had deposited a strip of sandy mud, covered with rounded grey stones. Around and about lay bits of cracked and dry wood, old sun-bleached branches washed down from wooded banks further upstream.

Sitting in the shelter of the willow our eyes could take in the finer features of the waterscape. On the outside of the bend, a miniature cliff face had been cut into the bank and, on top, brambles rolled like barbed wire. Insects drifted lazily about it in the still heat, the trees' thin leaves hanging motionless above. Against the dazzling blue sky and bright greenery, a solitary red kite patrolled his demesne searching for carrion. His silhouette still hovered as we turned away, an after-image with every blink. The beach of stones we sat on varied in grade from fine pebbles to fist-sized river cobbles. We picked them up and ran our hands over their smooth, weighty forms. Under the reach of the willow's branches was a line of three much larger rocks, the one nearest clearly projecting from the water, and the pair further out just breaking the surface near where the twisted roots emerged from the bank. These were perfect for the bracing and the gap on the far side between the rocks and the roots was a natural sluice for the stream to continue its journey. A blueprint was clear and, eager to cool down in the water, we struck on the idea of building a dam.

Off came boots and socks. With the hardy layer of tough rubber removed from our soles, the irregular stones in the bank became a sudden challenge, jutting uncomfortably or sliding unexpectedly beneath us as we flailed and tiptoed to the water. Its brisk coolness brought an immediate reward. There was a moment's shock at the first step, but the submerged stones were flatter, more comfortable than those on shore thanks to a soft cushion of weed. The current massaged our feet and the lapping of the surface around our ankles alternated warmth and cold as evaporation repeatedly stopped and started in the wavelets.

The fallen branches from our leafy parasol provided a good initial brace propped between the shore-bound and midstream rocks, and the best pieces of masonry were gathered from the stony shore. We concentrated on taking the filler material from just upstream of the dam, helping to deepen the rising pool already forming. The depth was threatening our rolled-up trousers, which had to be hitched further to an unfashionable and unflattering height. Like all good workmen, we stepped out occasionally to admire our handiwork, reading the changing flow and consulting on potential gaps or weak points, sucking air through our teeth for authenticity. The sense of momentum is great when people work together to solve a problem. At points we were consumed by individual tasks, but would look up to see the other, elbow-deep in the stream or tottering to the dam with the perfectly shaped stone to plug the next hole.

Eventually nearly four-fifths of the stream's breadth had been stilled. The pool was 6 or 7 centimetres higher than downstream, more than 20 deeper overall. The escape channel by the far bank was now a loud rapid as the entire water-flow gushed through less than a 30-centimetre gap. The impairment of the flow had quieted more of the stream than we expected. As the water by the dam found it could not progress, it flowed gently backwards, only to meet the onrushing force behind it. A clear line of separation emerged, a wrinkle in the surface folding into a sharp crease between the gentle eddy and the newly redirected course. In the calm slack pool we had created a miniature bath and, with all hope abandoned of keeping our trousers dry, we took turns to submerge ourselves in it, luxuriating in the cool water, stretching a toe over the line to feel the pull towards the overflowing cascade.

Many people carry an inbuilt aversion to physically getting into wild water. Even on a glorious summer day we shun the effort of undressing and dressing again, taking off our tightly laced-up boots. At first, it feels cold and can be an unfamiliar world to the uninitiated: weeds, larvae, scuttling invertebrates and slimy bottom-feeders. Once in, however, excitement floods the system, our bodies and minds soon revert back to the pleasure of being in water. It is, after all, our first state, what novelist John Cheever called 'the resumption of our natural condition'. You can see the change in people, from gritted teeth and the choruses of 'ooohs' and 'aaaahs' to the laughter and hoots of happiness. Once in, it is hard to get out. The pages of Roger Deakin's *Waterlog* are soaked with this pleasure. Adopting a 'frog's-eye view' swimming through Britain's wild waters, his words are a paean to the pleasure of a personal physical journey down through the nooks and crannies of landscape, the streams, ponds, rivers and lakes. Dams transform rather than transport, yet the intimacy we felt after working with the rocks, the mud and the water was just as powerful.

We dried off in the sun, peering occasionally into our pool as the silt settled. One of the great things about damming is the chance to observe wildlife as it floods into the world you have created, exploring the new edifice. The clarity was astounding, and a Petri dish of stream-life was soon ours to observe. Pioneering minnows appeared darting around the leisurely slack away from the current. A torpedo-shaped male stickleback followed,

its red belly an impressive tunic adorned for the spawning season. Less colourful was a dark, mottled-brown
fish. The swollen shape was recognisable, a bullhead,
reminiscent of an injured appendage and earning it the
common name of a 'Miller's Thumb'. It approached
cautiously, hugging the stream bottom, looking for any
caddisfly larvae unearthed by our digging. Watching it
probe the dam wall for food, we were reminded of the
legendary tale of the Dutch boy whose finger saved the
town of Harleem from a leaking dyke.

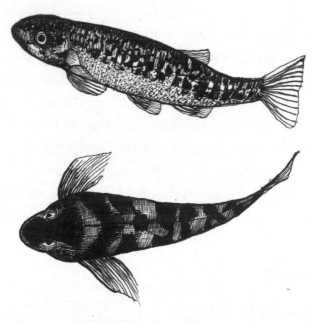

The lives of fish seem straightforward and fish tanks
have become a popular addition to our homes as much
for contemplation as decoration. Their reassuring, relaxing quality was used too in the first computer screensavers,
which presented scenes of piscine tropical beauty and

bubbling water sounds to assuage the unfamiliar absorption in technology. In reality, a simple bottle trap engages all the same positive effects. It is an easy and inexpensive way to get more closely acquainted with the inhabitants of our waterways, and meeting the locals certainly helps deepen our connection.

We pulled out one of our empty 2-litre plastic water bottles and cut the top off with a pocketknife about a centimetre below the point where it reached its full width. Inverted, this fit snugly back into the bottle and formed a neat funnel into an impromptu aquarium, which we placed beside the dam with the opening directed upstream. Attracted by a bit of bread from our sandwiches, the trap had its first colonials within twenty minutes, two sticklebacks nosing about the clear water. Pulled from the stream and placed on the bank, we watched this male and female blissfully unbothered by the huge, magnified, smiling faces on the other side of the bottle, gate-crashing their lunch date.

Dams have been an effective way of catching greater quantities of fish for thousands of years. Historians have found preserved examples dating back to the Mesolithic and, to this day, men of the Enawene Nawe tribe of western Brazil build vast wooden dams across the Amazon to trap fish during the wet season, an ancient ritual that remains vital to their survival. Aquatic engineering not dissimilar to ours also forms part of a fishing method widely used by the Kuki people of India, Burma and Bangladesh, whose dams divert the fish down sluice channels and into waiting woven baskets. But the impact and importance of dams spreads wider still. They have been a cornerstone of civilisation for millennia, improving farming irrigation and storing clean drinking water in dry seasons. Historically they have blocked water too, forming the defensive structure that holds back the sea from reclaimed lowlands, evidenced in the names of cities like Amsterdam and Rotterdam. Most recently, dams have been turned to producing hydroelectric power and holding reservoirs, allowing human habitation in even the most inhospitable places. Think of Las Vegas. Without the infrastructure of dams, levees and canals channelling supplies into our homes and on to our crops, our advancement and existence on this planet would be greatly curtailed.

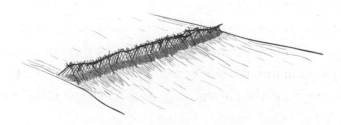

For those of us living in the developed world, there is really nothing natural about the way we get our water. It is seen less and less in anything approaching a natural state. We only ever seem to encounter it chlorinated, heated and filtered, stilled, distilled and vitamin-filled. It runs limitless from our taps and showers, but we have moved so far from being immersed in it, building our homes by it, relying on it for our food, that most people instinctively think of our natural rivers and streams as dangerous or dirty. Ironic that dams have to some extent created this divorce. But there is a human connection with wild water that Deakin sums up perfectly: 'You are *in* nature, part and parcel of it, in a far more complete and intense way than on dry land.'

The enjoyment we draw from it should never be to nature's detriment, however, and we carefully returned the sticklebacks to the stream. Fresh water must be respected and cared for, but this can only come through direct engagement. It has to be studied, enjoyed, swum in, waded through and played with to be appreciated. How else can we expect future generations to care? What relationships will they forge with our rivers, streams, brooks and ponds without the chance to experiment and fall in love with them firsthand? Watch any child feeding the ducks, trailing a toy boat on a string, or playing something as basic as Poohsticks on a stream and you can see their imaginative absorption into the landscape. As their stick races away at the mercy of the current they draw closer to the element da Vinci called 'the driving force of all nature'.

Poohsticks is a simple game, but exciting. Participants drop chosen twigs or other floating objects at an agreed point, and the first one to cross the finish line is the winner. Its simple appeal means it has never really gone away since being immortalised, when Winnie the Pooh 'thought that he would just look at the river . . . because it was a peaceful sort of day, so he lay down and looked at it, and it slipped slowly away beneath him, and suddenly, there was his fir-cone slipping away too'. A. A. Milne and his son Christopher Robin used either side of a bridge as start and finish and their original racecourse in Ashdown Forest has now been fully restored. There is even a world championship held at Day's Lock on the Thames in Oxfordshire.

Our dam provided a complex obstacle course to hone our skills, and the challenge was set. Agreeing whose stick is whose is sometimes tricky as they bob and twirl past one another. Ours were easy to distinguish, bits of hazel twig resembling an 'l' for Leo and an 'r' for Rob. The end of a stretch of shallow rapids upstream marked the starting gate, but we took quite different approaches, the 'r' going straight into the fastest part of the river, the 'l' into a gentler spot clearer of obstacles. The former raced ahead, but turned and even backtracked a little around a tufted mass of dock springing from the bank. We jogged alongside, willing them to use the speed of the open dash to the willow tree, but they drew side by side for a nail-biting finish.

It is remarkable how much personality our imaginations

can give something as simple as a stick in the water. Heading towards the speeding flow of the discharge channel around the dam, our agreed finish line, it looked for a moment like they might be swept into our pool and becalmed. But no, at the last second 'r' hit the folds of the current, accelerated away, and over the drop to clinch the win. In the end, 'l' never made it through the slalom gates of the willow roots and is probably lying there still; the first building block of a natural dam. Sometimes we wonder where our connection with nature has gone, but so many of our instincts draw us closer to it. All we need to do is step outside and play.

After the thrill of the race, we sat for a while with our feet cooling in the dam pool and dozed to the lulling lapping of the stream. A song thrush ran through its repertoire. From the west a light breeze rose and shook the long willow leaves as the brook murmured to itself. Few things are quite so peaceful as the sound of water. It is a noise so conducive to our calm that gurgling streams have become a signifier for tranquillity. Recordings of it are now sold on CDs and phone applications to cure insomnia and aid relaxation – Mother Nature as a best-selling artist. But a digital track only offers a flattened sense of the real thing. Nothing beats the live performance; the prickles of sweat from playing in the sun, feet cooled by a water feature you've worked to fashion, the lingering tingling of a vigorous foot massage from the pebbles.

Our environment returns the energy we invest in shaping it by shaping us back. By calming a stretch of water, we had calmed ourselves. We shouldn't have been surprised. This is in keeping with the idea of 'environmental determinism': that landscape and climate shapes society, culture, who and how we are. Gardening is an example of this. Some people cultivate shrubs from all over the world to get a colourful or exotic border that pleases the eye; others will cut down a tree to get a 'better' view. Both are altering what was there before, and both are projections of personal taste on to the landscape to create an aesthetic that changes the way we feel. Yet there is a tension between improvement and interference with the landscape. It can be seen in the way *Rhododendron ponticum* was once the height of fashion in Victorian gardens, an Eastern rarity to be envied, but it has since become a ubiquitous pest, impossible to eradicate and threatening to destroy native woods.

Since the Age of Enlightenment, reason has been applied to delineating areas of knowledge, separating and categorising the world. The 'natural' interrelatedness of humans and the environment faded into the background, lost among the bold new divisions: geology, botany, chemistry, physics – zooming in, we lost sight of the whole. Landscapes were tamed by aesthetic ideals. Capability Brown threw in lakes to improve a vista, parks were created with strategic stands of trees. He was following the philosophy of the day, that a heightened reflection of the glories of nature was the ideal. Writers of the period from Alexander Pope, to William Cowper to Jane Austen, linked character with landscape. A devious path represented deviousness of intent, an elegant garden spoke of an elegant owner. The desire to work on the environment, to alter it, seems to be consubstantial with our desire to develop ourselves.

Nowadays, sensibilities have changed and alteration of the natural landscape is more likely seen as contrived. As society's environmental consciousness strengthens, there is often a resistance to 'interfering', even when necessary. Dams themselves are a brilliant illustration of this tricky balance. They are often crucial to our existence but regarded as destructive because of their impact on an area. Yet it is naive to think we can just leave everything as it is now. Scarcely a square metre of Britain is truly untouched by humans and chains of events started by human action can affect even distant wildernesses; vast islands of plastic have formed in the centre of the Pacific Ocean, for instance. In some cases, the effects of man are not negative. Landfill sites can be turned back into wildlife sanctuaries for our rarest species; coppiced woodland supports a broader diversity of life than if left to grow unchecked; hedgerows planted by farmers to delineate and protect land are homes to unique ecosystems. Creation and destruction exist in a complex cycle.

The beaver is a 'keystone' species in many parts of the world, vital to a vast number of other beings. Their lumberjack tendencies clear swathes of living forest and block watercourses. Their dams also even out fluctuations in the water table, filter pollutants, moisten the earth for miles around and provide deep, still waters to support all manner of pond life that cannot live in fast-flowing streams. Gerald of Wales wrote of seeing their dams built on the Teifi in the twelfth century, the same river our chosen tributary ran into only 100 metres downstream. The fertility that abounded such dams, extending even after they had been silted over to form verdant meadows, may even have inspired early man to create dams for their own purposes.

Hunted to extinction in Scotland in the sixteenth century for their fur, beavers lived alongside us perfectly amicably for many centuries. Having wiped them out, we are currently reintroducing them to Scotland in a move opposed by many locals. They were a native species but there is understandable fear that there will be unintended consequences to their dams, as in Tierra del Fuego in Argentina where they ravaged the landscape.

Modern scientific advance is commonly seen as a force that distances us from nature, but when Western scholars first began to use this same approach, they were fusing the logical and mathematical with something deeply experiential and rooted in nature. What became science was once 'natural philosophy', the discipline of considering the world around us. Its roots delve into experiences any of us can engage with if we take the time. When damming, we gain an insight into this drive to discover how things work. It takes on a real, three-dimensional form, quite different from the classroom. We play with the water-flow directly; we understand through experimenting what engineering principles are required for dams to contain a force of water. If we, as a species, can balance scientific reason with the love of the natural world that it arose from, we will give ourselves the best chance of damming the flow of change: not stopping it, but marrying human intervention with the natural world.

Sadly, we could not linger in our crook of the stream indefinitely. The lateness of the hour surprised us. The sun was still well above the treetops, but time had come to strike the dam and restore the river to its former flow. We heaved the matter back into the depression it had come from. The mud and small stones shushed over our bare feet again. The larger pieces were returned to the shore, and finally the branches pulled free. The water would quickly level any remaining particles.

As we walked away from the stream, its chatter became lost in the cricket's buzz that fizzed through the June afternoon. We reflected on the language and lessons of nature and how much we have to learn if we only allow ourselves to listen. Shakespeare said it best: 'Tongues in trees, books in the running brooks, sermons in stones, and good in every thing.'

Walk in the wild

In our densely populated world it is surprising just how close most of us live to untamed spaces. Even the most 'developed' countries have areas in which nature has free rein, whether by accident or design. National parks, wildlife reserves and areas of outstanding natural beauty demark islands of the uncivilised; the rugged fringes that bring a sense of wonder to our wandering. Walking in the wild is about exploring and sleeping out in these places, forging a path that takes us deeper into the landscape and ourselves.

Hills and mountains provide a perspective and a challenge. Exploring any landscape at different times of the year is rewarding but, for us, autumn is the ideal walking season. The days and nights are still fairly warm, but not as dehydrating as full summer; there is a bit of a breeze to keep you cool and rain swells mountain streams with fresh, drinkable water.

Begin by surveying the land in two dimensions. A detailed map, preferably at 1:25,000 scale, is essential when heading into any territory and gives you the information you need to plan and prepare. Carried in a waterproof case, it needn't restrict your freedom to roam, but will act as a reliable guide and give you the bigger picture should you become disoriented. Even established walking routes with signposted paths can wrong-foot a wild walker during inclement weather. Sheep tracks that lead nowhere may seem like the right way unless there is something to crosscheck them with. Maps also allow you to set an itinerary, should you desire or require one. This can of course be adapted and altered once on the ground, but it pays to have an idea of your movements so that you can identify places for refilling supplies and setting up camp.

Trace a rough route that also takes into account the amount of daylight and lie of the terrain. Autumn tends to have between 11 and 14 hours of daylight per day, so err on the safe side and don't plan for any longer than 10 hours walking in every 24. Estimate your pace over even ground as approximately 3 miles, or 4.8 kilometres, an hour, but bear in mind that the terrain will usually be rough underfoot with alternating gradients. The 'Naismith Rule', laid down by mountaineer William Naismith in the nineteenth century, is to allow an additional hour for every 600 metres of ascent. This was created for other mountaineers, so take it as a maximum. Another more accurate method is to approximate that climbing a metre in altitude takes around eight times as long as walking it on the flat. So, whereas covering 10 kilometres on the flat would take around two hours, add a fairly modest uphill gradient of 500 metres over the same distance and the time is increased by 60 minutes. Look at the area you intend to cover, taking account of the contour information and using this equation to see if it is achievable.

Wild walking requires little kit: stout boots, sunhat, waterproofs, some warm clothes (wear layers as you may also be hot depending on the weather), a couple of litres of water per person, and food. Plan for a number of lighter, carbohydrate-rich meals and chocolate bars rather than pig-out picnics. Always bring extra rations in case of an emergency. If sleeping out, you will need a few more things: a sleeping bag, roll mat and tent if you aren't planning on building a den. Some people take weight-saving to extremes. It is possible to make a tarpaulin sheet double up as both waterproof poncho and single-layer tent, using walking sticks as tent poles and reducing the overall load. For most, though, a decent lightweight tent or bivouac bag is sufficient. Camping overnight means water requirements go up too so either double up supplies or pack water-purifying tablets and find a free-flowing stream on the map. Heartier food for the evening is also important after a day's exertions. Where making fire is prohibited take a small, portable stove. Cooking equipment can be kept light; you only need one small camping pan with a lid to boil water and a plastic fork/spoon will do for everything you can't eat with your fingers. Don't take plates; eat dehydrated package soups, noodles, stews or pasta dishes straight from a plastic cup. These are also the lightest dinners to carry.

Aim to arrive in the early morning and start by walking out at a steady pace, the weight of the rucksack balanced on your hips rather than your shoulders. A nice measure for a good walking speed is the 'tune and talking test'. If you are too out of breath to talk without gasping a little, you're probably pushing yourself too hard and will tire early. If you can sing without gasping, you're not going quickly enough to get the full health benefits.

Take in your surroundings. Identify something, a line of trees, rocky outcrop or river crossing, somewhere that is both on the map and in your field of vision. Make your aim to navigate to this landmark via the most interesting path. By breaking the walking into manageable sections you can regularly check that you are going the right way, but as you walk try to read the landscape and keep a general idea of direction. The sun and the wind shape nature and the reliability of these influences gives accurate bearings if you know how to find them. Wild walking means orienting as much from these signs as the map. Indeed, there is no quicker shortcut to grounding yourself in the terrain than learning how to navigate with natural direction indicators.

On a clear day, the sun is the most reliable. It rises in the east and sets in the west, of course, but anywhere outside the tropics it will not pass directly overhead in between. In the Northern Hemisphere it passes in an arc to the south, and will be precisely south at midday. You can work out the bearing on which it lies with great precision using appropriate charts and tables, but a reasonable rule of thumb is that dawn is east, sunset is west, midday is south, and the sun's bearing changes by 15° per hour in between. This occurs more slowly in the morning and evening because the sun is climbing or falling as well as progressing. Also, in winter it rises and sets almost south-east and south-west, and in summer this is almost north-east and north-west, because of the earth's tilted axis. Only on the equinoxes (around 19/20 March and 22/23 September, depending on the year) does it truly rise dead east and set dead west.

Trees can also act as a natural compass if time is taken to study the way they grow. Draw your judgements from a range of exposed trees rather than a single example, and be wary of any that may be affected by more immediate environmental conditions, such as buildings or other trees growing around it. Look at shape. There is usually a dominant wind in any given locality and if the wild walker learns this before setting out, they can get a good idea of their direction by noting how a tree has developed. In Great Britain, for example, the wind mostly blows from the west/south-west. On exposed trees in the mountains, its effect can often be seen in the way a trunk leans away from this direction, therefore pointing east/north-east. The influence may be more subtle, however: a straighter trunk but with the windward side of a tree developing fewer shoots, buds and branches, and the sheltered side blooming with foliage. This can also be seen in reeds, which typically develop flowers on the less windy side.

The sun's influence also stamps a directional indicator on certain trees. The 'tick' principle is that the side of trees that receives most sunlight (i.e. the southern side when in the Northern Hemisphere) develops noticeably greater amounts of foliage and more horizontal branches. On the northern aspect, the branches grow more vertically in the pursuit of light, giving the overall impression of a tick shape, with the long arm of the tick pointing south. Horse chestnuts are particularly good guides, as are beech, oak, maples and London plane trees.

The mass of trees all around us was less helpful. Sweat dripped off our noses on to tea-rose-tinted earth and stone scuffed from beneath the topsoil. We were climbing straight up the tumbledown stone steps through a dense copse of uniform firs, the wet wood, loud drips of rain and closeness of atmosphere lending a distinctly tropical air. It was far hotter than expected from the dire weather forecast. Spattering rain and dense cloud cover had suggested a jumper and waterproofs, but the stillness and the challenging slope were combining to poach us. Wordsworth called the Lake District 'a sort of national property, in which every man has a right and interest who has an eye to perceive and a heart to enjoy'. We had taken him at his word, but so far our eyes stung with sweat and our hearts were pounding with the effort.

At the top of the stone stairs, the trees stopped in a neat line. On the edge of the wood a few trunks had been felled recently and we saw a light egg-yolk yellow stump lying exposed to the elements.

NORTH

WEST

EAST

SOUTH

Native Americans used tree rings to navigate, observing that the core of the tree lies nearer the bark on the south side and that the bark of old trees is thicker to the north and north-east side. Leonardo da Vinci also noted this fact and our stump confirmed it. We were heading on a south-west bearing, up a twisting narrow track through waves of soggy, golden bracken. Scrambling onwards, our first milestone lay ahead: an ominous oval of water. The Ordnance Survey map showed Bleaberry Tarn nestled between the shoulders of two green-grey peaks, but we couldn't see them. They were cloud-cowled and invisible. Even at this early point we had taken hundreds of uphill steps, equivalent to continuous weighted squats, adding up to a serious workout. A moment spent assessing the next ascent was respite for our shaking legs.

The track vanished into the clouds at 45° and became indistinguishable from the surrounding rough reddish rock. After another 10 metres, there would be little in the way of landmarks save for the contours of the rolling mountains we stood upon. This brought an unsettling pang; we would only know the route we were taking was the right one by virtue of the fact that we wouldn't be falling over a sheer cliff.

Mercifully, the rain eased. We removed layers of fleece and waterproof, but it didn't stop another soaking from sweat as we began the next climb. Visibility soon reduced to no more than a dozen metres. The irregular ridge that wound up the mountain was sloped and tumbled. The world had become a small, grey bubble and any sense of height was lost as the cold, dark tarn rapidly faded from view. Through the dank mist shadows rose up at all sides. In a landscape that seemed to change shape as each new cloudbank blew across it, the grind of the climb and the red earth below our boots were the only things we could focus on without our heads spinning.

The path levelled and a man-high cairn signalled our arrival at the peak. Following tradition, we each added a stone before collapsing against it. The sense of satisfaction at having completed the bulk of the uphill walking planned for the day was leavened with the knowledge that this was only the first of several summits on a long ridge we were aiming to cover. A much more difficult navigational challenge lay ahead. Our aim was to circumnavigate the tarn far below, skirting the crags to the next peak. No path was visible. We couldn't see our destination. In fact, we couldn't see past a rusted iron post lying bent and twisted 20 metres away. Knowing from the line of ascent that the tarn lay below and to our left, we elected to keep the plunging cliff at a safe distance, but use it as a visible marker as we progressed along its edge. We were thankful that the sea of fog concealed the 200-metre drop and clouded any sense of vertigo.

This was the mountain's hinterland: a blasted top, punctuated by black rock and low tufts of hardy grass and heather. Strange, twisted iron posts poked through the wet earth in what must have been ordered Guardsman-like lines at one time. Now they sagged and lurched like drunks. Everything smelt wet and we threw on our warm layers and waterproofs as the sweat cooled on our skin. It was quiet. Only the wild, whining alarm of a bird somewhere rang out of the blur. Our advance was slow, and more than once the precipitous guiderail of ancient iron posts was lost from view completely in the misty cloud, leaving us for long stretches in a featureless level plain of dull, dark green, domed in ghostly grey. This was utterly disorientating. Turning back and heading straight towards the sheer fall was our only option at such times, as the cliff was the sole point we could cross reference with the map. We slowed our pace as we approached the edge to avoid strolling into a mention in the local papers. Our bearing restored, we pressed on resolutely but felt the twinge of nerves at our sight becoming increasingly more impaired.

Recording the distance you are travelling can be tricky with little visibility, but counting your paces is a good way to get an idea. With each set of ten steps, extend a digit on your hands. When all ten fingers are counted, pocket a small pebble or marker and start again. It takes, on average, 2,000 paces to a mile, depending on your height and the gradient you are walking. Start this technique at a landmark on a map such as a cairn, and you can correlate your estimated tally to find a rough position and work out where you are.

A darkening blur ahead seemed to indicate more rainfall, but gradually resolved into a great, exposed shoulder of andesite lava and granite that shrugged off the turf. It was an island in the silent storm. Combined with our DIY odometer, we could identify it as the gateway to the narrowest point along our ridge, with steep drops to either side. As we advanced gingerly, the mist brightened to a dazzling white, as though we were inside a pearlescent light bulb. It raised our spirits; the next climb might lead us out of the cover. But nature had a greater gift in store.

The clouds parted either side, like a pack of horses suddenly breaking and the racetrack emerging from between their massed bodies. We could see everywhere at once and found ourselves standing at the centre of a ridge joining two peaks and between two great valleys, framed by a backdrop of towering mountaintops. Each was as Wordsworth described, 'like some vast building made of many crags', their names resounding with lofty power: Great Gable, Pillar, Steeple. Sunlight lanced through the great herds of cumulus hanging weightless, lighting and shadowing the panorama. Opposite, a powerful stream; livened by the rains, it was a streak of fat intersecting a great haunch of muscular mountain flank.

Our eyes flowed from vista to vista, spoilt for choice, but then as we finally reached for cameras, another cloud rushed up the mountainside. It was huge; a cathedral of water vapour hurtling towards us at 30 miles an hour. We fell silent and watched helpless at its rapid approach, a rowing boat facing a mighty, onrushing storm wave of the Atlantic. The impact was silent, but wiped everything from view in an instant. We were submerged again.

The broadening ridge had lost its rapid decline to either side so we were again thrown on to our detailed contour-reading skills for orientation. Another line of skeletal posts might have marked a boundary line on the map, but it seemed to be in the wrong direction and much too close to the edge. The occasional squat tor sometimes sported a manmade cairn, but sometimes not. On this endless shallow plane we opted for going uphill continually, reasoning that we would arrive at our next destination, the highest peak in this set of fells, and could follow the footpath leading off it. Certainly gaining height would give the best vantage point for our next move.

The great thing about wild walking is that we walk inside our heads as much as we do through the mountains. This is quite different from walking in a built-up area, where external stimuli, the crowds, traffic lights, cars, adverts, vie for our attention. Unlike sedentary meditation, however, your body is fully active; there is no risk of torpor. The world passing by you and your thoughts interlace.

Wild walking in good weather is a blessing, but we had discovered that even bad weather can be an inspiration. Finding our way through obscurity naturally becomes a meditation on finding a path to any aim. None of us can see the ultimate end of anything we attempt and our view of even the near future may be vague and prone to misinterpretation. Navigating in the fog, we did our best to keep moving up and forward, and had to be content with progress being made little by little. Every step was a step through a bank of confusion. Divining our direction from the presence of particular lichens on one side of a rock was nigh on impossible in an unfamiliar world where myriad un-guessed factors could be at play. We had to reason our way out.

In *Purgatorio*, the Italian poet Dante made sure to employ all manner of realistic detail, like the exact angle of the sun for 9.30 in the morning, and the effect on the light as an all-encompassing mist dissolves. He linked it to the fog of anger, the only escape from which is reason, leading us to salvation, 'Sì come cieco va dietro a sua guida' ('as a blind man goes behind his guide'). Dante walked across much of Italy as an exile from his native Florence, and *Purgatorio* is as much a product of his physical experience of penance as an abstract theological work. The rhythmic tramp of feet as a source of inspiration was also favoured by Wordsworth who wrote of his fondness for composing during hikes through the very hills we were traversing.

It isn't surprising that pilgrimage comes to mind when wild walking. From long solo struggles along established trails to Jerusalem or Mecca, to the motley characters of Chaucer's *Canterbury Tales* or Kumbh Mela, which, at over 60 million, is the largest gathering of people in the world ever. There are modern pilgrimages too, to Graceland, to battlefields. Our minds seem inclined to value those things we have to work hard for. Pilgrimage on foot, or over a length of time, magnifies the goal with every step, preparing us for a powerful reaction when the journey is complete. It takes work to consider something free as priceless, and taking the time to observe and discuss each passing beck, rill, cairn and tarn helps us to earn every peak.

The target of our pilgrimage was not a religious site,

but was the favoured haunt of A. W. Wainwright, famous for his series of illustrated guides to the Lake District. He said: 'for beauty, variety and interesting detail, for sheer fascination and unique individuality, the summit area of Haystacks is supreme'. His widow even scattered his ashes over Innominate Tarn near the summit. As we approached Haystacks' north-west face, the cloud had dispersed completely, replaced by a bright sun. Searching for somewhere dry, sheltered and safe to pitch our camp, we ranged all over its craggy lid, stripped down to T-shirts and shorts. Not only were there a number of bodies of still water to watch out for, most of the ground was sodden and moss-rich, and we couldn't pitch on the bare rock; we needed to find an elevated, grassy place.

A wild campsite must be on a considered spot. It should be away from rivers that may swell, not underneath branches that may drop, and never too exposed to strong winds. Making a weaving advance is a good way to check a large area, and we set off at right angles to one another, mimicking the warp and weft of a net. Eventually the ideal location presented itself. A roof garden nestled between the rocky skyscrapers of the mountains, this flat lawn was encircled by purple heather that ran down to a little tarn, and was bordered by a rise of rock. Beyond the tarn was a sharp sweep away to the west, revealing the entire Buttermere valley in spectacular glory. We had pitched south-westerly to take best advantage and so that any wind would blow over the hull of our tent, its thinnest end turned into the oncoming waves like a ship.

With this done, our first action was to get a brew on. Bolstering the comfort and morale of anyone in the outdoors, a simple cup of tea, coffee or soup is as though the very sense of achievement has been made corporeal, warming and relaxing. The clouds we had climbed through split and rose, shadowing the peaks, but the valley end and the sea lay beyond, lit with a glorious sun, a vibrant golden stage.

A sunset is the wild walker's greatest reward. There is something righteous in the fact that only those willing to put in the hard work of the day's climb get to see the sun descend over these places. Regardless of wealth or status, such a view must be paid for with sweat and it was reassuring to think that only a small number of people would ever have watched night fall from this peak, most heading down into the villages for well-earned dinners before dark.

With shelter and sustenance provided, it is natural to explore the area around a camp in more detail. The tarn just below us mirrored the lighter sky at the foot of the valley, and by a trick of the perspective appeared vast, though in truth it was only half-a-dozen metres across. The rocky outcroppings above and around us were as rugged as any of the distant peaks, and the gnarled, wind-twisted heather resembled nothing so much as tiny oak trees, a bonsai woodland in the clouds. Meadow pipits were our only company and they picked about the heather, like dinosaurs stalking this miniature forest. Many of the forces of erosion that sculpt the largest peaks occur on every scale. Miniature landscapes are easy to miss against a spectacular backdrop, but slowing to look at them reveals that it's not just how many peaks you cover, but how well you cover them. When sleeping out, there is no rush to descend and we can spend longer looking, drawing closer.

In that moment, a curious thing occurred. All the planning, packing and perambulating had come down to this brief window of time. Rehydrated, well fed, with endorphins flowing from exercise and the spectacle of nature unfurling before us, the many slow steps that got us to this point seemed to compress into a headlong rush. Hours ago we were somewhere familiar, making rudimentary calculations in front of the worn sign of a pay and display car park. Now we were above even the weather.

Our day-to-day perspective on the world is usually fixed at a few hundred metres by brickwork and glass. When taking in the broader horizon of the mountains, the significance we place in our hustle-and-bustle lives is swept from our minds by miles of expanse. In the same way contemplating a fossil can reduce our greatest empires to an eye-blink; it can be exhilarating, unsettling or both. You might be content to take in the magnificence of nature, or realise that your greatest desire at this point is to find someone to share it with; you might feel driven like Wordsworth or Turner to express it through art. Breathing in the clear air, looking all the way to the sea, your heart might go out to people who do not have the opportunity to experience such freedom. Or perhaps you simply realise that you are perfectly content to be here, and will be equally content to return to the life in the valleys and towns below, enriched by the time spent aloft.

Psychologist Abraham Maslow described the euphoric feeling of connectedness and harmony we feel when everything comes together as a 'peak experience'. Maslow cites basic drives, such as food and shelter, which need to be met before we can advance to fulfilling higher needs. Wild walking involves carrying all our requirements on our backs. Our basic needs are all within arm's reach, packed into a rucksack. Their tangibility and proximity perhaps assuages the usual urges to meet them, allowing us a quicker route up to our own mental peak.

It has been suggested that pilgrimage could be a Jungian archetype – an experience every one of us can relate to because it is inherited in some whispered form from our evolution as a nomadic or migratory species. Maybe it draws its resonance from a time we can all barely remember, early childhood, when the desire to walk was a potent source of joy and frustration, not just a symbol of passage but a literal gaining of the ability to pass through into a new state. Whatever the underlying reason for 'taking a long walk' playing so strongly on our sympathies, its transformative power has led to its appearance time and again in story. John Bunyan's *The Pilgrim's Progress* has a cast of characters, each one an allegory for some positive or negative quality. The overarching metaphor is one that fuses time, space and spiritual advancement, with the journey of the protagonist, Christian, representing his passage through life and his struggle for salvation. Walking many miles takes many hours and provides ample time for reflection on existence, whatever your beliefs. Like Christian, our aching legs and shoulders told us that much of what we carry is unnecessary; we actually require very little as human beings to survive, physically or spiritually. Much of what we consider essential is just baggage that weighs us down during the tough ascents. There is nothing like wild walking to give you the desire to live more simply and become focused on the things that matter in life. No doubt this is why traditional rites of passage into adulthood required and continue to require similar rituals. Think of students taking a gap year, setting out with their backpacks to wander distant parts.

The Aboriginal Australian tradition of 'walkabout' is shrouded in mystery, the full significance only revealed to those who have undertaken the process. A component of this disappearance into 'the bush' and living in the wilderness for up to six months is recreating journeys ancestors and legendary figures took over the same ground during the mythic past of 'the Dreaming' or 'Dreamtime'. Encountering your ancestors when camping is perhaps unlikely (unless you brought your parents along), but sleeping out adds a huge amount to a day spent walking. It is more than simply extra hours in the outdoors. It alters your mindset when there is no rush to catch the last train home. There is a freedom that comes with setting out with enough in your pack to last you all through a day, two days, longer even, and knowing that everything is your decision. Climbing into a sleeping bag under the stars, you feel a liberation. There is a desire to continue wandering wherever you choose with no set end or particular destination in mind.

The next morning we strode off towards the rising dawn. We walked where we wanted over the fells in a bleaching sunshine. Filling our bottles from streams or cooking up soup in the woods, our choice was dictated by nothing more than our whim at any given moment to investigate a glimpsed glade or distant waterfall. When we returned from the mountains into the lush valleys of the lakes below, it was with a heightened sense of the physical world around us. Everything was compared with the scale of nature we had seen in that world above. The walk to the water seemed an easy stroll through the wood, a carpet of pine needles deep and brown cushioning our weary steps and creaking knees. Curiously, though, there was no sense of things failing to live up to the majesty of where we had been. It all seemed to fit together perfectly. Nature is a rich puzzle, some pieces mighty mountains, others gentle waters. Climbing up towards the sky, we had merely been to one of the puzzle's edges. It felt just as good stepping into a different-shaped piece.

A stream ran silvery down to the opposite shore, silent and stationary at this distance. Removing boots and socks from swollen feet, we walked across the gentle decline and into the cool, clear water. Our contentment rendered us dumb. Picking pebbles from below the glassy surface, we sent them skimming out into the vast expanse, breaking the reflected sky into a thousand shards.

Bibliography and
further reading

Anning, Mary, quoted in Dickens, Charles, *Mary Anning, the Fossil Finder* (13, All Year Round), 1865.

Baker, J. A., *The Peregrine* (Harper), 1967.

Ball, Phillip, *The Music Instinct: How Music Works and Why We Can't Do Without It* (Vintage), 2011.

Bang, Preben, and Dahlstrom, Preben, *Collins Guide to Animal Tracks and Signs* (Collins), 1974.

Beecher, Henry Ward, *Proverbs from a Plymouth Pulpit* (D. Appleton and Co.), 1887.

Beethoven, Ludwig van, Letter to Therese Malfatti, 1808, from *Symphony No. 6 in F major, op. 68, 'The Pastoral'* (http://www.all-about-beethoven.com/symphony6. html), 2004–2006.

Berman, Marc G., Jonides, John, and Kaplan, Stephen, *The Cognitive Benefits of Interacting with Nature* (http://www-personal.umich.edu/~jjonides/pdf/2008_2.pdf), 2008.

Bird, Dr William, as quoted in the article 'Mental health "helped by birdsong" ' by Arifa Akbar (*Independent*), 2007.

Birkhead, Tim, *The Wisdom of Birds* (Bloomsbury), 2008.

Bunyan, John, *The Pilgrim's Progress From This World to That Which Is to Come* (London), 1678.

Burne, Charlotte Sophia, *Handbook of Folklore* (Kessinger Publishing), 2003.

Cheever, John, *The Stories of John Cheever* (Alfred A. Knopf), 1978.

Clift, Jean Dalby, and Clift, Wallace, *The Archetype of Pilgrimage: Outer Action with Inner Meaning* (New York: The Paulist Press), 1996.

Collis, John Stewart, *The Worm Forgives the Plough* (Vintage Classics), 2009.

Csikszentmihalyi, Mihaly, *Flow: The Psychology of Optimal Experience* (New York: Harper and Row), 1990.

Dante, *Purgatorio*, trans. Robin Kirkpatrick (Penguin Classics), 2007.

Darwin, Charles, extract from *Letter to Joseph D. Hooker*, February 1871 (www.christs.cam.ac.uk), 2011.

Deakin, Roger, *Wildwood: A Journey Through Trees* (Penguin), 2008.

Deakin, Roger, *Notes from Walnut Tree Farm* (Penguin), 2009.

Deakin, Roger, *Waterlog: A Swimmer's Journey Through Britain* (Vintage, new edn), 2009.

Einstein, Albert, extract from *Letter to Margot Einstein*, 1951; quote by Hanna Loewy in *A&E Television Einstein Biography* (VPI International), 1991.

Gatty, Harold, *Finding Your Way Without Map or Compass* (Dover Publications), 1999.

Gooley, Tristan, *The Natural Navigator* (Virgin Books), 2010.

Grayling, A. C., 'What We Can Learn from Nature' (*The Times*), 2009.

Hughes, Ted, *The Hawk in the Rain* (Faber & Faber), 1957.

Jefferies, Richard, *Nature Near London* (Chatto & Windus), 1883.

Jefferies, Richard, *The Gamekeeper at Home and the Amateur Poacher* (Oxford University Press), 1960.

Kant, Immanuel, *Critique of the Power of Judgment*, trans. and ed. Paul Guyer and Eric Matthews from *The Cambridge Edition of the Works of Immanuel Kant* (Cambridge University Press), 2000.

Keats, John, *The Complete Poems*, ed. John Barnard (Penguin Classics), 2003.

Krutch, Joseph Wood, *The Twelve Seasons* (Ayer Co. Publishers), 1949.

Kyriakidis, Evangelos, *The Archaeology of Ritual* (Cotsen Institute of Archaeology, UCLA publications), 2007.

Leakey, Richard, and Lewin, Roger, *Origins Reconsidered: In Search of What Makes Us Human* (Anchor), 1991.

Louv, Richard, *Last Child in the Woods* (Atlantic Books), 2010.

Mabey, Richard, *Food for Free* (Collins, new edn), 2001.

MacEnery, Father John, as cited in Stringer, Chris, *Homo Britannicus: The Incredible Story of Human Life in Britain* (Penguin), 2006.

Macfarlane, Robert, *The Wild Places* (Granta), 2007.

Macfarlane, Robert, *Mountains of the Mind: A History of a Fascination* (Granta, reprint), 2007.

Malafouris, Lambros, 'The Cognitive Basis of Material Engagement: Where Brain, Body and Culture Conflate', appeared in *Rethinking Materiality: The Engagement of Mind with the Material World* (Cambridge: McDonald Institute for Archaeological Research), 2004.

McGonigal, Jane, *Reality Is Broken: Why Games Make Us Better and How They Can Change the World* (The Penguin Press HC), 2011.

Maslow, Abraham, *Religion, Values and Peak Experiences* (New York: Viking), 1964.

Mears, Ray, *The Outdoor Survival Handbook* (Ebury), 1994.

Milne, A. A., *The House at Pooh Corner* (Methuen & Co.), 1928.

Pfister, L., Savenije, H., and Fenicia, F., *Leonardo da Vinci's Water Theory: On the Origin and Fate of Water* (International Association of Hydrological Sciences), 2009.

Pretor-Pinney, Gavin, *The Cloudspotter's Guide* (Sceptre), 2006.

Pretty, Jules, Griffin, Murray, Sellens, Martin, and Pretty, Chris,
Green Exercise: Complementary Roles of Nature, Exercise and Diet in Physical and Emotional Well-Being and Implications for Public Health Policy (CES Occasional Paper 2003–1, University of Essex), 2003.

Rackham, Oliver, *The Medieval Landscape in Essex*: *Archaeology in Essex to A.D. 1500*, edited by D. G. Buckley (London), 1980.

Radcliffe, William, *Fishing from Earliest Times* (John Murray), 1921.

Shakespeare, William, *As You Like It* (Penguin/Godfrey Cave paperback edn), 2007.

Steinbeck, John, *The Log from the Sea of Cortez* (Penguin Classics), 2001.

Stringer, Chris, *Homo Britannicus: The Incredible Story of Human Life in Britain* (Penguin), 2006.

Tzu, Lao, *The Book of Tao and Teh*, trans. Gu Zhengkun (Peking University Press), 2006.

Wainwright, A. W., *A Pictorial Guide to the Lakeland Fells, Volume 7: The Western Fells* (Westmorland Gazette), 1966.

Walton, Izaak, and Cotton, Charles, *The Compleat Angler: Or, the Contemplative Man's Recreation* (Coachwhip Publications), 2005.

Wordsworth, William, *A Complete Guide to the Lakes*, ed. John Hudson (Longman), 1846.

Wrangham, Richard, *Catching Fire: How Cooking Made Us Human* (Profile Books), 2010.

Websites

http://www.shipwrecks.uk.com
http://www.scribd.com/doc/58601334/2/POP-GUN
http://www.treesforlife.org.uk/forest/mythfolk/elder.html
http://www2.btcv.org.uk
http://www.childrenandnature.org

Acknowledgements

Writing this book has been a journey for us both, one that could never have been completed without the patience, understanding and unstinting love and support of our families and friends. To them we owe everything.

Also deserving of special mention are Steph Ebdon and Jessica Wollard at The Marsh Agency, who provided us with the guidance and good advice that helped bring our ideas to fruition; Mark Booth at Coronet/Hodder who had the foresight to commission the book and was instrumental in shaping its form and encouraging us to get to the point; Charlotte Hardman for her diligence and dedication in making sure everything got done on time; and everyone at Coronet whose hard work and belief in the importance of a connection to the wild ensured this book was written, and written in the right way.

This book owes a great debt to writers who have blazed a trail for nature literature, from Richard Jefferies to the late Roger Deakin. In particular we were inspired by Jefferies's *The Amateur Poacher* and *The Gamekeeper at Home*, and J. A. Baker's *The Peregrine*. Robert MacFarlane's wonderful and evocative *Mountains of the Mind* and Deakin's *Wildwood* and *Notes from Walnut Tree Farm*, released shortly after we conceived the idea for this book, showed us what we could aspire to and draw inspiration from. We are doubly grateful to the Society of Authors for awarding us the Roger Deakin grant, both for supporting the completion of the book and for showing us that we might be living up to his memory in some small way. Though we never had the chance to meet him, we drew close to him through his words and felt his presence when sleeping out in the woods and sitting by the rivers. We are also indebted to Ray Mears, whose expertise and dedication to espousing the benefits of traditional lore continues to enhance the perception of wild spaces as enriching their visitors and to make them accessible to all.

Thanks also to Ben Ross at *The Independent* who believed in the book from the off and gave us the space to publish some of our ideas in a monthly column while we were also writing this book. Similarly, to all the kind strangers who offered encouragement through the newspaper and our website. Your words were a great motivation.

We are unable to acknowledge everyone who helped us make our journey, but special mention must go to those who mentored, fed, accommodated and assisted us as we travelled and researched this book: Ed Bassett of EB Adventures, Wayne Jones and all at Forest Knights, Gerald, Tessa, Agga and Lawrence Price, Pearl Myers and the Myers family, Peter and Jane Hoole and the Hoole family, Dom and Steph Turner at Skiology, Alan Jones of Shipwrecks.uk.com, Laura Hoppit, Tina Fotherby, Sarah Turner at Transworld, the team at Skillsmart Retail and Chris and Rose Bax at Taste The Wild. We would also like to give a special mention to (for Rob): Mum, Dad, Karen, Matthew, Natalie, Freya, Niamh, Tim Jones, James Westropp, Charles Westropp, Peter Westropp, Alex Corbet Burcher, Phil Westerman, Will Ridler, Drew Johnson, George Welsh, Jordan and Alanna Frieda, Lizzie and Danny Varian, Amy Sebire, James Yuill, Olly Samuel, John Stevens, Danny Williams, Max Lawrie, Joe Johnson, Matt Bagley, Si Skirrow, Rob Menzer, Jim Kean, Fiona and Geoff Scholtes, Katie Sotheran, Will Warbrick, James Nelmes, Nick Monkhouse, Paul Schofield. (And for Leo): Mum, Dad, Matt and Ruby, Kevin Atherton, Salley Vickers, Claire and Tim Regis, Richard Mott, Ed Whiting, David Salçedo, Zillah Myers, Will Watson, Chris Simons, Nikhil Gomes, Alistair South, Tim Muttukumaru, Will Jobling, Colin Cornforth, Jane Gilbert, Hamer Boot, Martha Newell, Sean Farrington, Tom Walters, Dave and Rosa Tough, Dan Matlin, Robin Vandome, Katie Playfair, Tom Lumley, Ben and Katie Joyce.

Finally, those whose efforts put us in the position to write and illustrate this book in the first place: Christopher Wallbank, Peter Jolly, Mike Parkinson, Martin McQuillan, Marcel Swiboda, Simon O'Sullivan, all at Leeds University, Jon Newton, Gavin Alexander, Robin Kirkpatrick, Freya Johnston, Malcolm Garret, Issam Kourbaj.